SIDORE NEWMAN
SCHOOL
1903

$6.00
SIGNED
1ST ED

D1087145

# ISIDORE NEWMAN SCHOOL

## ONE HUNDRED YEARS

# ISIDORE NEWMAN SCHOOL
## ONE HUNDRED YEARS

ANNE ROCHELL KONIGSMARK

NEW ORLEANS 2004

This book is not meant to be a comprehensive historic document but rather the
story of a wonderful school.  We apologize for omitting anything that should have been included.
We trust that we have made fair use of available sources.

© 2004
Isidore Newman School
1903 Jefferson Avenue
New Orleans, LA 70115
www.newmanschool.org

First edition. 5000 copies

*Library of Congress Cataloging-in-Publication Data*
Konigsmark, Anne Rochell
    Isidore Newman School : one hundred years / by Anne Rochell Konigsmark
      p. cm.
    ISBN 0-9747959-0-9

Design by Michael Ledet Art & Design, Hammond, LA
Typography by Eugenie Seidenberg Delaney, North Ferrisburgh, VT
Color Separations by Garrison Digital Color, Inc., Kolleen Herndon, Consultant, New Orleans, LA
Print Management by Kaye Alexander, Castle Hill, VT
Printing by Friesens Book Division, Altona, Manitoba, Canada

*FRONT COVER: The Gottesman Gate, the entry gate at Isidore Newman School. Photo by Richard Sexton.*
*BACK COVER: Original school building, on Peters Avenue, known as the Jefferson Building since the street
became Jefferson Avenue in the 1930s. Valmont Building is in the background.  Photographer unknown.*

Printed in Canada

*ENDLEAVES: Jefferson Building of
Isidore Newman School, photo by
Kate Elkins.*
*FACING THE TITLE PAGE: Jefferson
Building, photo by Richard Sexton.*
*RIGHT: Cotonio Palaestra, photo by
Richard Sexton.*

# CONTENTS

*LEFT: A bridge leads to the Lower School complex. Photo by Richard Sexton.*

*Newman students donned Isidore Newman masks at a Founder's Day program honoring the ninety-fifth birthday of the school. Photo by Matt Rose. Copyright 2003 The Times-Picayune Publishing Co., all rights reserved. Used with permission of the Times-Picayune.*

# PREFACE

THIS BOOK IS THE RESULT of a year of intense research, using materials from Newman's own extensive archives, documents from the Historic New Orleans Collection, the newspaper collections of the New Orleans Public Library and memories and information culled from more than 150 interviews with alumni, parents, teachers and administrators.

Many Newman people, places and events are in the pages of this book, but far more people, places and events are not documented here. Hard choices were made, and undoubtedly, important details have been left out. Moreover, this book was written from one perspective — that of an outsider looking in. I hope you will read this book as a celebration of the spirit of Isidore Newman School, and forgive the omissions and flaws. We have not attempted to identify students in the photos. The photos were selected not for the students shown but because they represent an activity or era in the life of the school.

It has been a delight getting to explore Newman's glorious past and reflect on its bright future. This school truly stands alone in New Orleans, and this book is meant to tell the story not only of the school, but of its role in the city it calls home. It is a record of a school within a city within a century.

I am grateful to the members of the book committee — Phyllis Alltmont, Nancy Bissinger, Susan Good, Carol McCall, Scott McLeod, Genie McCloskey, Joan Starr and David Stone — who hired me and met with me every month for a year to provide guidance and support. They gave me their trust, and they gave me absolute artistic freedom; working with them has been one of the most pleasurable experiences in my career as a writer.

Newman could not have produced such a beautiful book without the expertise of Michael Ledet, who also gave me much-needed encouragement throughout the process. Herman Kohlmeyer Jr., Isidore Newman's great-grandson, provided vital family history, as did William Rosen, a descendant of Rabbi Isaac L. Leucht. Thanks to all the interviewees who opened their hearts and their homes to me; their contributions make this book the vibrant, colorful story that it is.

And without Genie McCloskey's well-organized archives, her institutional memory and her undying school spirit, well, there would be no book. Many thanks to the woman in green!

ANNE ROCHELL KONIGSMARK

ix

*Portrait of Rebecca Kiefer Newman, Isidore Newman's wife.*   *Portrait of Isidore Newman, founder of Isidore Newman School.*

# STATEMENT OF PURPOSE

Newman values each individual.

Newman is committed to the intellectual, ethical, emotional
and physical development of each student.

Newman instills in each student the School's core values of honesty,
kindness, respect, and responsibility, and develops in each student
self-confidence and an appreciation for cultural and personal differences.

Newman offers a challenging, comprehensive and sequential curriculum
from pre-kindergarten through twelfth grade, one which encourages
creativity, critical and independent thinking, and different ways of learning.

Newman promotes academic excellence and celebrates
participation and accomplishment in the fine arts and athletics.

Newman engenders in each student the skills, attitudes, and character
necessary for productive lifelong learning and service to others.

# TIMELINE

**Feb. 28, 1837** — Isidor Neumond is born.

**Nov. 7, 1853** — Isidor Neumond comes to America — his name changes to Isidore Newman.

**1856** — Jewish Orphans' Home opens on Chippewa Street.

**1887** — The Home moves to 5342 St. Charles Avenue.

**May 4, 1902** — Isidore Newman offers money to establish a manual training school for the children of the Home.

**1903** — Isidore Newman Manual Training School is established and construction is underway. Mr. Newman is awarded the Picayune Loving Cup for endowing the school.

**October 3, 1904** — First day of school. James Addicott is first principal.

**January 8, 1905** — Dedication ceremony at the school. Rabbis from Atlanta, Shreveport and Galveston speak. New Orleans Mayor Martin Behrman attends.

**1907** — On Mr. Newman's seventieth birthday, his sons and daughters donate a substantial fund for school improvements. A school tradition is established: Founder's Day. Mr. Newman is given a silver replica of the school.

**1907** — A new building is built facing Valmont Street to house the elementary grades.

**1908** — Harold Weil graduates in a class of one. Principal James Addicott leaves, and Vice-Principal Clarence C. Henson takes his place.

**1909** — The first commencement is held. Mr. Newman gives to the school land bordered by Valmont, Franklin, Saratoga and Dufossat streets. Isidore Newman dies.

**1910** — At the first Founder's Day without Isidore Newman, a marble tablet is unveiled: "In Memoriam of Isidore Newman, Founder and Friend of This School. His Life's Crowning Deed."

**1911** — First issue of the *Pioneer*, the student-run magazine, is published.

**1914** — Class of 1915 gives a fountain to the school. It remains in front of the school today.

**1917** — The Isidore Newman Manual Training School Endowment Fund, set up by Mr. Newman's family, is used to construct a new, three-story building facing Saratoga Street. It is used for arts and sciences. C.C. Hayden becomes principal.

**1918** — First free-standing gymnasium is constructed. J.W. Curtis becomes principal. Influenza epidemic delays opening of school by a month. Commercial Department added to school under the direction of Mr. L. A. Davidson: courses in shorthand, bookkeeping, typing, business English, and commercial arithmetic are offered.

**1919** — Mr. Henson returns as principal. The first Alumni Association is formed, and a parent-teacher group is organized. Mr. Newman's wife, Rebecca Kiefer Newman, dies.

**1922** — First of G. Campbell Cooksey's operettas is performed.

**1924** — Harold Weil, Newman's first graduate, enrolls his daughter, Therese, into kindergarten at Newman. The first crop of second-generation Newman students is called "Manual's Grandchildren."

**1930** — Newman celebrates its silver anniversary. The *Pioneer* wins first place in a national contest sponsored by the

Columbia Scholastic Press Association of Columbia University. Newman is the first school in Louisiana to be accepted in the Southern Association of Colleges and Secondary Schools.

1931 — School name changes to Isidore Newman School.

1933, **Founder's Day** — Mrs. J.K. Schwartz, oldest daughter of Isidore Newman, presents the school with a portrait of her father.

1936 — The *Pioneer* announces the arrival of the school's first "trained librarian," Louise Hoehn. She takes inventory and finds 280 books are missing.

1939 — Mrs. Edwin Neugass, a daughter of Isidore Newman, presents to the school a bust of Mr. Newman that she sculpted herself.

November 1941 — The first Homecoming.

1945 — Dads Club is founded.

1946 — Jewish Children's Home closes.

November 21, 1946 — Newman school is incorporated as a separate, non-profit entity with its own board of trustees.

1947 — Clarence Henson retires. He is named Director Emeritus. Eddy Kalin, a faculty member since 1925, succeeds him as principal.

1948 — The school's first fund drive raises $125,000. Campus sees many improvements and renovations, including new science labs and a motion picture projection room. The Stern Building is completed, thanks to a $150,000 gift of Percival Stern and the Percival Stern Foundation in memory of Mr. Stern's parents.

April 6, 1950 — Students take the first Newman field trip to Washington, D.C.

1950 — The first Alumni Day.

1951 — A modern gymnasium is built with money from an anonymous donor. Land is purchased on Danneel and Valmont streets and Valmont Street is closed to traffic. The Dads Club raises money for the old gym to be converted into a girls' gym and a soundproof band room.

1951 — Marvin Durning, class of 1945, is named a Rhodes Scholar.

1953–54 — Newman celebrates its fiftieth anniversary.

1954 — Advanced Placement courses are initiated. The *Greenie*, the first student newspaper, begins publication. First Annual Fund campaign kicked off.

1955 — Basketball team wins Newman's first state championship. It is the first of nine championships for the basketball team.

1956 — Newman begins participating in the National Merit Scholar Program.

1961 — Newman becomes the first New Orleans school to have a microfilm reader in its library. Henson Auditorium opens. Lemle Building opens.

1962 — Clarence Henson dies.

1963 — Girls' swim team wins first of eight state championships.

1964 — William Cunningham becomes headmaster. Mr. Kalin is Director Emeritus.

1965 — Jefferson Building's red brick façade is painted ivory.

1966 — Cum Laude chapter is established at Newman.

1967 — Heymann Science Center is built.

1968 — Newman desegregates. It is the first private, non-parochial school in New Orleans to do so. Newman begins publishing *Absinthe*, a yearbook, in place of the "senior number" *Pioneer*.

1970 — First computer course begins, using a computer shared with several schools and a local business. At the time, computers cost as much as $50,000.

**1973** — Bertha Marcus Levy Student Center is built. Lower School building at the corner of Loyola and Jefferson avenues is built.

**1976** — Boys' tennis team wins the first of five state championships. Mr. Cunningham resigns and Teddy Cotonio becomes acting headmaster.

**1977** — Mr. Cotonio is named permanent headmaster.

**1978** — Newman gets its charter from the National Forensics League.

**1979** — First Newman Invitational Forensics Tournament. Walter Isaacson '70 is named a Rhodes Scholar. The first two endowed chairs are established: Joseph C. Morris Chair in Science/Mathematics and William B. Wisdom Chair in English. ACTIONS replaces the Philanthropic Club. Seventy-fifth anniversary campaign to raise $5 million.

**1980** — Computers installed in business, admissions, administration and development offices. And they are used to teach computer science in-house.

**1980** — Former Newman Principal Eddy Kalin dies. In September, vandals burn six swastikas into the lawn in front of the Jefferson Building. When those were covered up with green paint, four more appear. In 1981, there are at least ten bomb scares at Newman, more than at any other local private school.

**1981** — Palaestra opens.

**1982** — Girl's gym becomes Charles Keller III Fine Arts Center. Boys' gym named for Edward "Skeets" Tuohy.

**1983** — Girls' tennis team wins first of two state championships.

**1984** — Girls' gymnastics team wins first of two state championships. For the first time, there is a campus security guard, and more fencing around campus. Childcare program for faculty opens in a renovated shotgun house on Dufossat Street — later named the Greenie House.

**1985** — First color yearbook is published. Michael Lupin Field opens. Volleyball team wins first of fourteen state championships, more than any other Newman team. Boys' golf team wins first state championship. Newman is recognized as one of 281 exemplary schools in the United States by the secretary of education. It is one of only seventeen private, non-sectarian schools chosen.

**1986** — Headmaster Teddy Cotonio dies in a car wreck en route to a basketball game. Theodore Cotonio III Chair in Humanities established. Humanities course established.

**1987** — Michael Lacopo is appointed headmaster. Palaestra renamed in honor of Mr. Cotonio.

**1989** — Lower School uniform adopted. Girls' cross country team wins first of four state championships.

**1990** — Summerbridge begins. Boys' cross country team wins first of two state championships. Newman Parents Association's office established on campus.

**1993** — Mr. Lacopo resigns. Scott McLeod is named interim headmaster. Newman wins National Physics Olympiad. Boys' soccer wins first of four state championships.

**1994** — Scott McLeod is named Newman's ninth headmaster. The school celebrates its ninetieth birthday. New mission statement is crafted. First line says it all: "Newman values each individual." Anthony Reginelli Chair in Physical Education established. First Wonder Week.

**1995** — First pre-kindergarten class begins. New pre-kindergarten building opens. Justin Osofsky '95 wins the National Forensics League national tournament for the Lincoln-Douglas debate.

**1996** — There is now a computer in every classroom on

campus. Philip Skelding '92 is named a Rhodes Scholar. He is the third one in Newman's history.

**1998** — Boys' swim team wins first of four state championships. Core Values are introduced: honesty, integrity, respect and responsibility.

**1999** — Master Plan completed. Girls' soccer wins first of three state championships.

**2000** — Dining hall and mini-theater in the Bertha Marcus Levy Building are renovated. Usdin Family Patio created. Fine Arts Week begins. Boys' baseball wins first of two state championships.

**2001** — Berger Family Fitness Center opens.

**2002** — Gottesman Entrance and Lawn and Philipson Health Center open. Original Stern Building demolished.

**2003** — School celebrates its centennial anniversary. A new Lower School complex, including the David Oreck Building, the Percival Stern Early Education Center and the Lupin Kindergarten, is dedicated. Lower School Building is named for Doris Zemurray Stone '29.

*A silver replica of Isidore Newman Manual Training School, given to Isidore Newman at the first Founder's Day celebration in 1907. It is on display in Newman's Rebecca Grant Popp Library. Photo by Garrison Digital Color, Inc.*

# CHAPTER ONE

# We are Newman

~⧫~

*ALMA MATER*
*In the southland's fairest city,*
*Reared against the southern sky,*
*Proudly stands our alma mater,*
*As the years go passing by.*
*Onward ever be our watchword,*
*Truth and honor will prevail.*
*Cradle of our youth's endeavor,*
*Newman School, we proudly hail.*

A. J. GUMA

I T IS LATE OCTOBER, it is unseasonably warm and it is threatening to rain. In the girls' room near the Henson Auditorium, young women set aside green pom-poms to pull their hair into long, curling ponytails. Seniors in high heels and dresses compete for a glimpse in the mirrors. Outside, in the hall, boys begin filing into the sloping, dark auditorium, their hands rammed into deep pockets — unless they are throwing friendly jabs at each other. Some older boys walk awkwardly in jackets and ties, their faces revealing a combination of discomfort and pride in their own good looks.

It is Homecoming 2002 at Isidore Newman School. The big game, the dance, the sense that high school is reaching its crescendo. The dressed-up students are members of the Homecoming Court, and the green-clad cheerleaders are preparing to rally the school to victory against Buras. The auditorium fills with enough kids to cause a riot, but as the queen, her maids and the escorts process down the aisles to the stage, there is reverent silence. Upper School Principal Jeff Brock reads off a litany of achievements; each student walks with artificial slowness to give him a chance to read them all. They are language and math whizzes, football and volleyball stars, hospital volunteers,

*LEFT: Class of 2003. Photo by Mike Posey Photography.*

club leaders, Summerbridge teachers, National Merit semifinalists, yearbook staffers, band captains, artists and actors. They are the Class of 2003. They are Newman.

It is a quintessential Newman moment, classic and timeless. You can almost see the bobby socks and pomaded hair of an earlier era. For those of you in the audience who wore bobby socks at Newman — or bell bottoms, or miniskirts — times like these make you cry, much to your consternation. They fill you with nostalgia, a sense of belonging and pride. You are amazed at how much things can change and yet stay so much the same.

You feel all this, even though most days you enter the auditorium without looking at the portraits that hang on the walls just outside. You may not even know who those people are behind the foggy picture glass. But their spirits fill this place. They came before bell bottoms, before bobby socks, long before this auditorium, but they are why you are proud to belong here.

Between the two auditorium doors is a portrait of the hall's namesake — Clarence C. Henson. Bookish, stern, with high ideals for what a school should be and how children should grow and learn, Mr. Henson was a Columbia University-educated, Ohio farm boy who came to the school as vice-principal and history teacher when it first opened in 1904. As a teacher and later as principal from 1908 to 1947, he shepherded Newman through the decades of its infancy and adolescence. He embraced academic excellence and taught social responsibility; he abhorred laziness and disdained snobbery. He is largely responsible for the firm foundation Newman stands on today.

*TOP: Cheerleaders in 2002. MIDDLE LEFT: Members of the football team in 2002. MIDDLE RIGHT: Scott McLeod, Newman's headmaster since 1993. BOTTOM: Homecoming Court in 2002.*

On the opposite wall, there is a picture of Margaret Turner Grout, a demanding, terrifying and beloved English teacher from 1928 to 1969. For generations of Newman students, she was the very essence of what a teacher should be. And there were others like her in those early days: career teachers in sensible shoes who demanded flawless grammar, who made Shakespeare come alive, who taught French and math skills that would last a lifetime. Many alumni say that no subsequent teachers — no Princeton chairman, no Harvard superstar — could hold a candle to teachers like Mrs. Grout.

In a heavy gilt frame, so high up on a wall that it's easy to miss, is a painting of the founder of the school, Isidore Newman. Mr. Newman — a distinguished man with a penetrating gaze — started life in America as a German immigrant teenager with one hand-sewn suit. He became wealthy and influential throughout the South, and he gave away money as naturally as most of us guard it. One of the last causes he championed was this school. He and other members of the Jewish community living in New Orleans around 1900 wanted the children of the Jewish Orphans' Home to have a private school that would equip them for useful and meaningful lives. He offered as much money as it would take to make it so.

Mr. Newman's money came with a few strings attached, and one of those strings gave the school a staying power no one could have predicted at the time. He said this place should not be a "Jewish" school, or an "orphans'" school. It should be a New Orleans school. It turned out to be the first — and for many years the only — co-educational, non-sectarian, college preparatory school in the city. In 1968, it would be the first private, non-parochial school to open its doors to black students.

The idea took: almost from the day the doors opened, the best and the brightest wanted in.

TOP: *Portrait of Isidore Newman.* MIDDLE: *Margaret Turner Grout, English teacher, 1928–1969 and chair of the English Department.* BOTTOM: *Clarence C. Henson, the school's first assistant principal from 1904 to 1908 and principal from 1908 to 1947.*

Mr. Henson, Mrs. Grout, Mr. Newman. They set the bar high, for themselves and for others. They are Newman.

Back inside the auditorium, midway through the 2002 Homecoming assembly, a Newman alumna, Katherine Fausset, class of 1993, gives a funny speech about how her alma mater comes to her in times of need, in the form of old classmates popping up at unexpected times, or a college professor asking where she went to high school, and being impressed by the answer. She is not yet thirty, but she is an author whose book, *The Cooking Club Cookbook,* caught the attention of NBC-TV's *Today.* She is poised. She is accomplished and at ease with herself. She is Newman.

Later on Lupin Field in a driving rain, Scott McLeod, Newman's headmaster since 1993, stands behind the goal post and watches water-logged cheerleaders keep a clutch of students in the soaked stands cheering their lungs out for the Greenies. Newman wins, 41-7. He is overwhelmed with admiration for the students on the field and those in the stands. He may be from California, but his school spirit can't be washed out in a little Louisiana thunderstorm. Mr. McLeod loves his students, and he will show them and tell them again and again, empowering them with his enthusiasm. He is Newman.

Founder's Day 2003. The Cotonio Palaestra, named for one of Newman's most beloved headmasters, is filling up with children, pre-teens, young adults, teachers and staff. The music from the band is deafening, rousing. At each set of doors is a display of large, black and white photographs of Newman in its first years. There are pictures of boys in woodworking class-

*Genie Everett McCloskey '65, a former Newman teacher and Newman's archivist.*

rooms, and girls in athletic sweaters emblazoned with an "M," because the school was originally Isidore Newman *Manual Training* School, and taught such practical life lessons as cabinet-making, sewing, mechanical drawing and cooking. The name, and the mission, changed in 1931. In the center of the arena is another display, honoring Isidore Newman and festooned with green balloons and green hearts, because it is also Valentine's Day. His portrait has been removed from its place in the lobby of the Jefferson Building and sits on an easel. A silver replica of the school — given to Mr. Newman at the very first Founder's Day in 1907 — is below the portrait on a table. The lights inside the little building still work and glow yellow from the shiny silver windows. There's also the original letter Mr. Newman wrote pledging the money to establish this school. It resurfaced just a few weeks before Founder's Day after years, maybe decades, of being lost, and it was quickly put in an elegant frame in time for this occasion.

Standing by an exit in a green blazer, clutching a camera and holding back tears, is Genie Everett McCloskey '65. A former Newman teacher, a Newman alumna married to a Newman alumnus, and a mother of three Newman graduates, she is now Newman's archivist. Without her, this display would not exist. She spent a decade organizing mountains of papers, files, photographs and memorabilia that had been sitting neglected in an office above the cafeteria. Every year, on Mr. Newman's birthday, she visits his grave in Metairie — alone. She leaves a large arrangement of flowers and picks up any stray trash that might be lying around. Her love for

*Girls in athletic letter sweaters, which until 1931 featured an "M" for "Manual."*

Newman — school and man — is hard to match. In honor of the institution that has been her second home for fifty years, she wears green every day. "Perhaps more than anyone in our community, Genie understands how important the past is to what the school is now," says Mr. McLeod.

She is Newman.

Founder's Day is a time to honor teachers, administrators and maintenance and kitchen staff — those who have been at Newman five years, ten years, thirty years. As Mr. McLeod reads off the names of these long-timers, kids erupt in ear-splitting applause. Some honorees get standing ovations. Young and old, star students and strugglers, the serious and the rebellious, are spontaneous and genuine in their show of respect and gratitude for the faculty and staff. They are Newman.

After the awards, band leader Michael Guma '66 leads everyone in the singing of the school song. Mr. McLeod asks A. J. Guma Sr. to stand; Mr. Guma resurrected Newman's fallow band in the 1940s, and led it until his son took over in 1978. He also wrote the school song. He's in the audience this Founder's Day because his daughter, Mary Virginia "Ginger" Guma '63 is receiving her award for twenty-five years of teaching. In one family, they are Newman's past, present and future. They are Newman.

It is May 27, 2003, a balmy and beautiful night in New Orleans. The seniors gather outside the Henson Auditorium for the last time, and line up to process to the stage. It is awards night, and the night before commencement. The students, in coats and ties, dresses and heels, look different than they did just seven months ago. There is something — what is it? The girls aren't playing with their hair or crossing their arms across

*LEFT: A.J. Guma, Newman's band director, 1942 to 1978.*
*RIGHT: Mary Virginia "Ginger" Guma '63, daughter of A.J. Guma and a Newman teacher for more than twenty-five years.*

their bodies. The boys have straightened their shoulders and their hands rest comfortably at their sides. They all look . . . *taller*. They are becoming men and women. And they are leaving.

The seniors settle themselves on risers on stage. They sing "America the Beautiful" — a high note is missed and a giggle is shared, but they continue to face forward and finish the song. Marc Kossover '87 is the teacher chosen by the graduating class to speak tonight. He tells a story about blowing up his driveway when he was a first-year teacher at a different school. He was trying to recreate an experiment Newman teacher Pierson Marshall — who is famous for blowing things up — performed when he was in school. While unsuccessful, Mr. Kossover says, his own experiment was an example of "Discimus Agere

Agendo," Newman's motto, which means "we learn to do by doing." "We expect our students to get their hands involved," he says. "This is an essential part of the Newman experience."

Mr. Kossover uses his mistake to teach that one should not just *do* things without thinking first. One should research ideas thoroughly, using the Internet, textbooks and classmates. "The life of the mind has its advantages," he says. Why does Newman win in sports, even when the other team is bigger, or stronger? Because Newman athletes know how to think, he says.

Students then receive awards for science, Spanish, math, sports and acting. The awards are named for a century of friends, alumni, former teachers and staff of the school. There's a public speaking award named for Clarence C. Henson, a band award named for A. J. Guma, and a singing award named for George Campbell Cooksey, the chorus director who for decades staged annual operettas. Forty seniors — almost half the class, receive the Zelia C. Christian award for attending every year at Newman. It is named for a teacher and assistant director who served Newman for thirty-eight years. There are Francis Soyka Cups for tennis, named for the beloved tennis teacher who taught generations of Newman students to "keep zee eye on zee ball." And finally, the oldest and most distinguished award, for citizenship, is named for Rebecca Kiefer Newman, in honor of Isidore Newman's wife. Since 1912, this prize has been given to a boy and girl who demonstrate the best school spirit and endeavor. In 2003, it is given to Janine Ho Moreau and Carter Thomas Davis. The prize is just one of many citizenship awards given to students for their loyalty, enthusiasm, character, community service, leadership and school spirit.

The next night is the ninety-fifth annual commencement, at Tulane University's McAlister Auditorium. Commencement has been here for fifty years, and for as long as anyone can remember, it has been on a Wednesday night in late May or early June. The boys wear rented white dinner jackets from Perlis and the girls wear long white dresses and carry small bouquets. They mill around outside McAlister Auditorium as the summer light softens and day blends into dusk. No one hates parents today; girls borrow lipstick from their moms and allow them to adjust their slips. Boys welcome hugs, even from younger siblings. They assemble on the steps for the photo. Meanwhile, because there are so many large, extended Newman families, commencement is like a reunion. An old woman approaches a younger woman to say hello.

"Who are you here for?" one says.

"My niece," says the other.

"A great nephew," the first replies.

"We just keep going through these Newman graduations!"

"And we've got a lot of little ones coming up!"

Mrs. McCloskey rings a bell to signal the start of the program. The seniors process to the stage. They sing "America the Beautiful," they listen to speeches, and they receive their diplomas. They leave the auditorium between two columns of almost 200 faculty, who clap and cheer proudly.

Most details are timeless: McAlister Auditorium, the dresses, the rented suits, the twilight, the singing of "America." Some are new: the bell ringing began in the 1990s, as did the tradition of graduates exiting between two rows of applauding faculty. For decades, the graduates went from commencement to a formal dance and midnight supper at the Lakewood Country Club; even the band, Deacon John and Ivories, was the same most years. Tonight, the young adults will party at a local club. This night honors the past, celebrates the present and embraces the future.

This is Newman.

*Detail, A mural, commissioned by Newman and created in 2003 by Tony Green, celebrates the school's first one hundred years. Here, founder Isidore Newman is seen in front of the Jewish Orphans' Home with children from the school.*

# CHAPTER TWO

# A School with an Ideal

Any man with wealth at his command can build a
school of physical bigness, of technical efficiency; but it
takes a man of vision to create what Isidore Newman
wished this institution to be — a school with an ideal!

RABBI EMIL W. LEIPZIGER,
*Founder's Day, 1919*

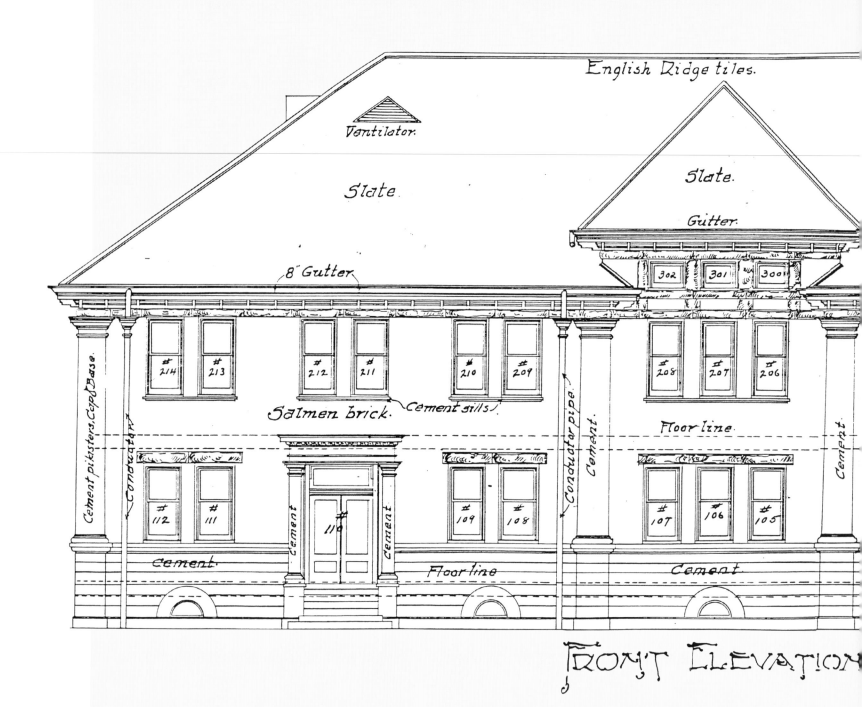

English Ridge tiles.

Ventilator.

Slate.

Slate.

Gutter.

8" Gutter.

Salmen brick.

Cement sills.

Cement pilasters, Cop'd Base.

Conductor

Conductor pipe.

Cement.

Floor line.

Cement.

# 214   # 213   # 212   # 211   # 210   # 209   # 208   # 207   # 206

302   301   300

Cement.

Cement.

# 112   # 111   # 110   # 109   # 108   # 107   # 106   # 105

Cement.   Floor line.   Cement.

FRONT ELEVATION

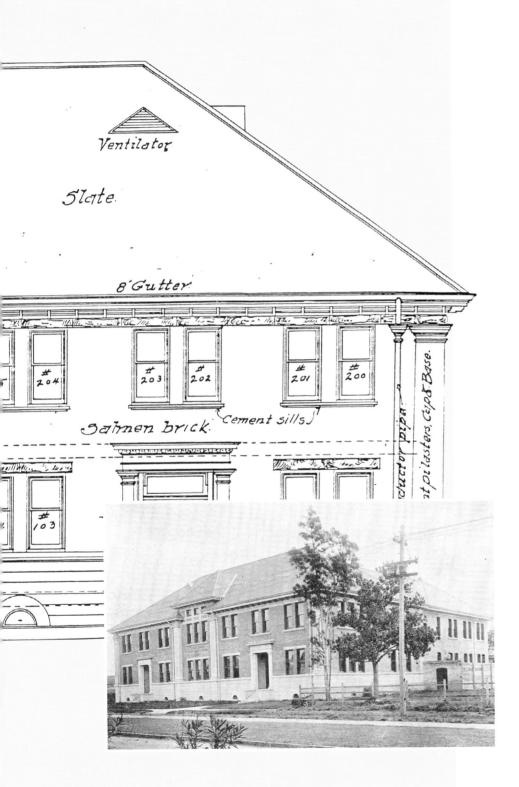

OCTOBER 3, 1904 was a warm but pleasant Monday in New Orleans. At 8:20 A.M., James Edwin Addicott, a California native, a graduate of Columbia University in New York, stood at the front doors of a brand-new building on Peters Avenue, now Jefferson Avenue. He looked down the street, residential then, as now, with stately, two-story houses and a neutral ground studded with palm trees. He watched as 102 boys and girls walked two-by-two from the Jewish Orphans' Home, three blocks away at 5342 St. Charles Avenue. Mr. Addicott also waited for twenty-three children from private homes.

It was the first day of school all over the city, and opening day for Isidore Newman Manual Training School. The lone school building was red brick, had two sets of doors on the front, and backed up to fields and woods. It was Mr. Addicott's first day as a principal, and the temperature was approaching eighty degrees as he stood waiting. Will the children be on time? Will there be order or chaos? Is anyone sick? Are the teachers qualified? Will the children be able to find the bathrooms, the gymnasium

LEFT: *An architect's drawing by the firm of Favrot and Livaudais of the first school building, 1903.* INSET: *Isidore Newman Manual Training School when it consisted of only one building. (From* The Story of the Jewish Orphans' Home.*)*

on the second floor, their homerooms? Mr. Addicott and his staff of eleven had seen to many details that day. One teacher was assigned to the boys' cloak room, another to the girls'. Homeroom teachers sat behind new desks in clean, unused classrooms. They were probably nervous, and prayed for a breeze to come through the transoms over the doors.

It was an important day, and, it turns out, a historic one. For New Orleans, it was the start of an experiment in a cutting-edge education method called manual training, which combined industrial skills-building with a traditional curriculum. For the teachers and staff of "Manual," as it quickly came to be called, it was the first day at a new job. For 125 students in eight grades, it was the beginning of a school year at a strange and unfamiliar place. They were an unusual assortment, from Jewish children living in an orphanage to Jewish and non-Jewish children from middle and upper class private homes.

And for a New Orleanian named Isidore Newman, a wealthy and well-known elderly man, it was the day his most satisfying philanthropic act bore fruit.

A few days before the school bearing his name opened its doors, Mr. Newman and his wife, Rebecca Kiefer Newman, sent a telegram to Mr. Addicott: "Our best wishes for the success of the Manual Training School. May it be the means to establish many more in our state and city as to enable our poor boys and girls as well as others to earn an honorable livelihood."

The motto of the new school was Discimus Agere Agendo. We learn to do by doing.

In a way, Isidore Newman School's beginnings go back half a century before it opened. On November 7, 1853, Isidor Neumond, a sixteen-year-old from Kaiserslautern, Germany,

immigrated to New Orleans in the steerage section of a sailing ship. United States Customs listed him as a farmer. He had blond hair, blue eyes, a passion for music and, legend has it, not a penny to his name. He was met by an uncle, Charles Newman, who had been in the city since 1828.

Isidore Newman — his name was Americanized — was one of 53,000 Germans who landed in New Orleans that year. The city was the second largest port of entry for immigrants

## DISCIMUS AGERE AGENDO

into the United States before the Civil War and the largest city west of the Appalachians. Many of the immigrants would continue on to other parts of the state or the country, but thousands stayed. By 1860, there were 20,000 Germans living in New Orleans. Their numbers were rivaled only by the Irish.

New Orleans, a hectic port city, suffered its worst epidemic of yellow fever in 1853. It began in late May and by the time it was over, some 10,000 people had died from the mosquito-borne disease. A third of the population of 150,000 fled town. Cemeteries were overflowing: people were buried in mass graves and shallow graves, often making unexpected and unwelcome reappearances during heavy rains. But by fall, the epidemic was a memory, and Isidore Newman landed in a thriving, prosperous city, its economy fueled by commerce on the Mississippi River, its population replenished by a constant influx of immigrants.

Isidore Newman's uncle and his four sons had a currency

RIGHT: New Orleans from the Lower Cotton Press, *detail*. (*From the Historic New Orleans Collection, 1947–20.*)

exchange business, but the newest arrival was sent to work in a general store in a Catahoula Parish town called Harrisonburg. Isidore Newman worked hard in the small town and saved enough money to send for his two younger brothers, Henry and Charles. The three of them established Newman Brothers cotton brokerage. The business did not last long; the economic devastation of the Civil War ended what was already a shaky venture. This was the last time Isidore Newman would have an unsuccessful business.

He returned to New Orleans and became a bookkeeper for his first cousin's husband, Henry Stern, who owned a wholesale shoe business on Canal Street near the river. Once he was back on his feet, Mr. Newman went into investment banking, while his brothers went into the cotton business. Isidore Newman's business was at 27 Camp Street. In 1868, he married Miss Rebecca Kiefer, a Mississippi woman who had lived across the river when he was in Harrisonburg. Where Mr. Newman was a quiet, steady man, Mrs. Newman was dynamic and commanding, even though she was only four and one half feet tall. He and his wife would have eight children, seven of whom lived to adulthood, and they spent many years in a Romanesque mansion on St. Charles Avenue at Foucher Street designed by the famous architect Thomas O. Sully. It was torn down in 1972.

Mr. Newman and his brothers grew very wealthy, and Isidore Newman became involved in many large-scale public and private ventures. He helped Louisiana and other southern cities and states recover from the Civil War by issuing soundly financed bonds. When a panic hit Wall Street in 1873, sending the country into a deep depression, Mr. Newman helped keep New Orleans and Louisiana afloat by cashing the scrip the bankrupt governments paid their employees. In the late 1870s, he provided financing for levee construction. In 1877, Mr.

Newman was a founding member of the New Orleans Stock Exchange; he later served as its president.

Mr. Newman was always looking for ways to enrich the Southern economy, especially after the Civil War. He knew the cities of the region needed to be electrified and modernized to catch up with their northern sisters, so in the 1890s, he acquired

*Isidore Newman's home at St. Charles Avenue and Foucher Street. It was torn down in 1972. (From the Historic New Orleans Collection, 1979.20.60.)*

nearly all the streetcar lines in New Orleans, and then bought the Edison Electric Company to electrify them. He did the same thing in Birmingham, Alabama; Little Rock, Arkansas; Nashville, Tennessee; Memphis, Tennessee; and Houston, Texas. He merged all except Nashville into one company, called American Cities Railway and Light Company. He also reorganized the Maison Blanche department store.

Isidore Newman donated money generously all his life. He gave with no fanfare, often sending money with a note that

16

*The first Maison Blanche building, shown when electric streetcars began traveling New Orleans streets.*
*(From Vieux Carre Survey, Sq. 94, Don Leyrer, the Historic New Orleans Collection.)*

simply said, "Enclosed please find check." He gave $2,000 every year to finance free concerts in Audubon Park, and erected an outdoor bandstand there in 1904. Beginning in the 1880s, he established a tradition: two days before Christmas and two days before New Year's, he would have one of his sons bring him the city directory and read aloud the list of charitable institutions. He would then call out where he wanted checks sent, basing his decision solely on who needed it most and who seemed worthy. He donated money to Jewish, Christian and black institutions. In his will, he mentioned twenty-eight charities. It is estimated that he gave away about $2 million over his lifetime.

Isidore Newman served on the boards of several charitable organizations. In 1874, he was elected to the board of directors of the New Orleans Association for the Relief of Jewish Widows and Orphans, and he and his family would hold various positions within the organization for decades. It was his involvement with the association that eventually led to the creation of a school in his name.

The Association for the Relief of Jewish Widows and Orphans was formed in 1854 after the Hebrew Benevolent Society, then one of the two main Jewish charities in town, called a mass meeting of New Orleans' Jews to address the urgent needs of those left widowed and orphaned by the 1853 yellow fever epidemic. There were about 2,000 Jews living in New Orleans in the mid-1850s. The new association, with money donated from Jews and gentiles, opened a home at the corner of Chippewa Street and Jackson Avenue on February 1, 1856. One widow and her five children, as well as seven orphans, moved in. It was the first home for Jewish orphans in the United States.

By 1885, after more epidemics and the Civil War, the population of widows and orphans at the home had grown to more

*Reverend Dr. Isaac L. Leucht, a rabbi and first vice-president of the Association for the Relief of Jewish Widows and Orphans. (From* The Story of the Jewish Orphans' Home.*)*

than one hundred, and they needed more space. The Association for the Relief of Jewish Widows and Orphans bought land at St. Charles and Peters avenues for $8,500 and hired architect Thomas Sully to design a spacious and child-friendly home. The entire project, including the land, cost $100,000. In 1887, the widows and orphans moved in; three years later, the widows were moved to Touro Infirmary and later to another home, and the St. Charles Home served children only.

At first, the Home employed a teacher and the children had their lessons there. Later, they attended public schools, although the Home supplemented their outside education with tutors. But the Reverend Dr. Isaac L. Leucht, a rabbi and first vice-president of the Association for the Relief of Jewish Widows and Orphans, didn't think the orphans' education, in particular that of the boys, was preparing them adequately to find jobs and make their way in the world. In 1889, he addressed the association's annual meeting and said that while the girls were getting a good

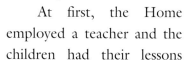

*RIGHT: Jewish Orphans' Home (from the Historic New Orleans Collection, 1970.29.43)*

education in the public schools — and, thanks to the recent addition of a "matron" at the home, they were learning housekeeping — the boys needed something more. Rabbi Leucht said:

*I am strongly of the opinion that, in the near future, something must be done enabling our boys to enter a useful career, as mechanics, and this can only be reached by an Industrial School, wherein the dormant faculties of our boys may be developed, and a love of trade may be instilled. I deem it to be one of the most sacred aims of this Institution, not simply to feed, clothe, rear and shelter its wards, but to fit them for life and its struggles.*

Rabbi Leucht was a prominent religious leader in New Orleans in the late nineteenth and early twentieth centuries. A Reform rabbi originally from Germany, he held positions at various synagogues, and was the first lifetime rabbi at Touro Synagogue. He was active in countless New Orleans and Louisiana governmental and charitable organizations: the Young Men's Hebrew Association was organized in his home and he helped raise funds to build Touro Infirmary. He was a member of the state Board of Education, he was president of the Red Cross Society and he was one of the first people in Louisiana to take supplies to the survivors of the 1900 hurricane in Galveston, Texas.

Throughout the 1890s, the notion of an industrial school came up repeatedly at the board meetings of the Jewish Orphans' Home. In 1895, it was reported to the board that an orphans' asylum in Cleveland, Ohio had created a school for its children that had adopted, with great success, a new education method called manual training. Manual training, a precursor to vocational training, is thought to have been developed by Swiss

educator Johann Heinrich Pestalozzi (1746–1827). It didn't replace a traditional curriculum; it only added to it. Training children in such trades as metalworking and woodworking, sewing and cooking, the theory went, enhanced not only the

Touro Synagogue, New Orleans, La.

*A postcard depicting Touro Synagogue (from the Historic New Orleans Collection, 1959.2.200).*

students' employment opportunities, but also their minds. American educators learned of it when officials from a school in St. Petersburg, Russia demonstrated a form of manual training at the Centennial Exposition in Philadelphia in 1876. John Daniel Runkle brought what he had seen there to Massachusetts Institute of Technology. In 1879, Calvin M. Woodward, considered to be the father of manual training in the U.S., opened the Manual Training School for boys in St. Louis, Missouri. The idea became popular in part because of the need for trained workers after the Civil War. But educators were attracted to it as a tool for intellectual development. By 1900, manual training was a part of the curriculum in dozens of city school systems, as well as in many private schools, such as the Harvard School for boys in Los Angeles.

When Isidore Newman Manual Training School opened in 1904, Principal James Addicott explained the little-understood concept to *The New Orleans Times-Democrat*:

> *The Manual training school does not attempt to teach any particular art or trade. What it does attempt is to educate the hand as an invaluable and necessary aid in the development of the brain. The great object is to teach the pupil to work as well as to think; to enable him to do something with his hands as well as to answer questions, and this instruction in the use of the hand demands and develops not manual dexterity alone, but attention, observation, judgment and reasoning.*

Manual training fell out of favor by the early 1920s; it was crippled in part by its name, which made it sound very un-intellectual. Vocational schools sprang up to take over the business of training children who would not or could not go to college. The federal government began funding vocational and industrial schools during World War I, in part out of fear of German supremacy. As early as the 1910s, Isidore Newman Manual Training School was becoming a college preparatory school, even though the words "manual training" would not be dropped from the school's name until 1931.

But in its heyday, manual training was an especially appealing option for the children of the Jewish Orphans' Home, as it would give them skills they might need to make a living. In the spring of 1902, the Home board invited Gabriel Bamberger, who ran a manual training school for poor children

in a predominantly Jewish Chicago neighborhood, to appear before the board. Some board members had been skeptical about manual training, but once they heard Mr. Bamberger speak, they were convinced of the need for such a school for the orphans. Only two questions remained, according to a 1905 account called *The Story of the Jewish Orphans' Home*:

"The first: Shall we take our wards away from public schools, away from contact with other children, for the purpose of giving them this admittedly superior education?

"Second: Have we the means to establish and conduct such a school?"

On May 4, just a few weeks after this meeting, Isidore Newman wrote a letter to the board of directors offering all the money necessary for the establishment of a manual training school:

> *Appreciating your noble efforts for the past ten years to erect a training school for boys and girls, and having read the able and convincing address of Mr. G. Bamberger, I have concluded to offer to you the money requisite to erect such a building, and hope that Providence may spare you to see this building completed, and enable the boys and girls of our city to derive the full benefit of your labor.*

On May 18, 1902, Rabbi Leucht wrote a letter to Newman, thanking him in his customarily florid prose:

> *. . . in accepting your munificent gift, in the name of our Home, we beg to convey to you that we consider it one of the grand deeds performed upon the battlefields of humanity, where poverty and ignorance are successfully overcome, and where enlightenment and progress will forever unfurl their victorious banners.*

Isidore Newman made several requests for the school that would bear his name. It would be for both boys and girls, he said, and there would be no uniforms, even though at the time, that was pretty much all the Home children ever wore. He didn't want to stigmatize them or have them stand out at this new school. He asked that the students receive a well-rounded liberal education as well as manual training. He stipulated that classes in music, art and citizenship be required. Mr. Newman's son, Jacob Kiefer Newman, donated money for instruments, so the children could form a band. Physical education would be offered.

Finally, Isidore Newman made an important request: He wanted the school to be open to children from private homes, regardless of their religion. In the segregated South, it did not even need to be said that the school would be for white children only. Decades later however, Mr. Newman's inclusive spirit was invoked when the Board of Governors decided to make Newman the first private, non-parochial school in New Orleans to integrate.

Things moved quickly from there. On July 6, 1902, the association purchased land on Peters Avenue for $8,500. By the end of 1903, the building was almost complete. Rabbi Leucht and Mr. Newman traveled to New York to hire a principal from Columbia University's Teacher's College. They chose James Edwin Addicott, who had studied manual training, and offered him $3,000 a year. They told him to choose a vice-principal, and he brought along Clarence C. Henson. It was estimated it would cost about $12,000 a year to run the school. By the time the school opened in October, 1904, Mr. Newman had given it $75,000.

Because the school was to be the first manual training school in New Orleans, and because it would be open to the

*Clarence C. Henson, principal of Newman from 1908–1947.*

community, Mr. Newman's gift attracted attention. In 1903, he was awarded the prestigious Picayune Loving Cup for committing "the worthiest act of 1902." The gift of the school was "practical in the extreme," according to an article in the *Times-Democrat*. He was the second person ever to receive the award.

According to the paper, Mr. Newman said it was New Orleans that had made it possible for him to be wealthy, so it was only natural that he would want to give something back to the city.

"While our Jewish community expects to realize to a great extent the benefit derived from this undertaking, yet it is pro-

*Class of 1913.*

posed also to receive gentiles," Mr. Newman said. "This, no doubt, will redound our reputation for liberality, and convince the community that we are not clannish or sectional."

Rabbi Leucht said:

> *I have never heard [Isidore Newman] say "No" when requested to do his share in relieving distress or to lead in an enterprise for the public good. His crowning benefaction, to erect a manual training school for the orphans of the Jewish Home, was accompanied by the request that an equal number of non-Jewish children be educated in its walls. "I believe," he said, "that a co-education in this direction will do a great deal to diminish prejudices which yet exist."*

As these and other statements reveal, Rabbi Leucht and Mr. Newman were committed to breaking down barriers between religions. They did not limit their civic involvement to Jewish charities and organizations. Rabbi Leucht called himself a devotee of "unsectarianism," and he passionately believed America would be the place where people of different creeds finally would stand

*TOP: Sewing class at Isidore Newman Manual Training School.*
*BOTTOM: Print shop at Manual.*

on common and equal ground. Rabbi Leucht called America the Promised Land because he envisioned all religions living together here in peace. "Men should stand together irrespective of religious belief," he once said. "I am a Jew and yet am also a Protestant and also a Catholic. For I always protest against anything that opposes light and progress, and I am universal in my belief in the fatherhood of God and the brotherhood of man."

Two of Rabbi Leucht's close associates were well-known Protestant ministers: the Reverend Dr. Benjamin Morgan Palmer, pastor of the First Presbyterian Church, and the Reverend Dr. Beverley Warner, minister of Trinity Episcopal Church. When Rev. Palmer died, his congregation asked Rabbi Leucht to deliver the eulogy. The friendship of these three highly respected men was both a reflection of and an influence on the relationship of Jews and non-Jews in New Orleans at the turn of the century. As Mr. Newman said, prejudices did exist, but New Orleans, and the state as a whole, historically had been open and accepting of Jews. They were some of the earliest settlers in the region, and they were elected to high offices earlier than in most states. In the nineteenth century, Jews were in the elite Boston Club and helped found the Pickwick Club. The first Rex, or king of Carnival, in 1872 was Jewish.

But in the late nineteenth century, anti-Semitism was on the rise all across Europe, and was intensifying in the United States. There was a famous incident in 1877 at Saratoga, New York: the Grand Union Hotel, an exclusive resort, turned away a very wealthy and well-connected Jewish man, and made national headlines as a result. At the same time, there was division among Jews in New Orleans. When large numbers of Jewish immigrants, escaping deadly persecution in Eastern Europe, began arriving in New Orleans in the late nineteenth century, many of the established Jewish families from Germany

and Alsace did not want to associate with them. Most of the new arrivals were Orthodox, unlike earlier Jewish immigrants like Mr. Newman, who were Reform. The earlier Jewish immigrants had made a point of melding into their new community. The new immigrants had distinct traditions, foods and ways of dressing that set them apart. Many were poor and uneducated. They were isolated by the older Jewish families, who feared being associated with a group that seemed unlikely to blend in as quickly as they had. That could explain why Mr. Newman, upon receiving the Loving Cup, said he hoped the gift of the school would prove that Jews weren't "clannish."

By the early twentieth century, the New Orleans social clubs, including the Boston Club and Mardi Gras krewes, were excluding Jews. John M. Barry writes in his 1997 book, *Rising Tide,* that around 1913 or 1914, Rex, who traditionally stops his float along the parade route at "suitably important places," passed up the Harmony Club, which was Jewish, for the first time. Jews and socially prominent gentiles remained friends and business partners but, Mr. Barry writes, "a line had been drawn."

Meanwhile, Newman School became and remained a place where the children of socially segregated parents mixed. Both gentile socialites and established Jewish families sent their children to Newman. It was a haven of inclusiveness, especially for the younger children. Society and its distinctions did creep inside the school walls as the boys and girls became teenagers and those who were socially connected joined organizations that excluded their Jewish classmates. Many Jewish alumni say they hardly noticed, but some say they felt a sting of rejection. Still, many friendships endured, and bonds that were formed in the protected world of Newman lasted a lifetime. Often, those children grew up to become prominent and influential New

*Isidore Newman was presented with the 1903 Picayune Loving Cup for funding a manual training school for orphans and other New Orleans children. It was deemed "the worthiest act of 1902." Photo by Garrison Digital Color, Inc.*

Orleanians, forming law and business partnerships or getting involved in the same charitable organizations. These bonds perhaps softened the hard line of exclusivity drawn by Mardi Gras krewes and social clubs.

Just as the friendship of Rabbi Leucht and the Protestant ministers both reflected and influenced how New Orleanians of different creeds got along at the turn of the century, Newman School could be said to have done the same. "The school has provided a bridge between Jews and non-Jews in the city, and it has been a great mediating force in our city," said Andree Keil Moss '55. "It has built friendships that have lasted."

Rabbi Leucht said in a 1907 article in the *Times-Democrat,* after paying a visit to the school:

> *Ah! Those who daily come here and see how these children mingle with each other, eat, drink, play and learn together, and observe how friendships grow and ripen between them, may behold the beginning of the coming of the millennium in this commonwealth, when a human being will no longer be asked, What dost thou believe? But, What art thou? Art thou good and honest, true and strong?*

On September 30, 1904, four days before Isidore Newman Manual Training School opened, the faculty met in Mr. Addicott's office.

"On account of the excessively warm weather, only matters of prime importance were discussed," read the minutes, recorded in fountain pen in a bound, lined ledger. Mr. Addicott instructed his staff to try to keep the school tidy, since everything was new. He gave them advice on how to teach: "Carefulness and reasonable accuracy are to be required. Kindness and firmness are to go hand in hand." At subsequent meetings that fall, he made some other suggestions, the minutes say:

"Use a low tone of voice and do not talk too fast. Do not overlook misconduct in students . . . Train for observation. Induce students to think and in every way make the influence of school felt at home."

At the first meeting, the vice-principal, Clarence C. Henson, laid out the history curriculum:

**First year**: *primitive life*
**Second year**: *early myths*
**Third year**: *local history*
**Fourth year**: *"stories" of American life*
**Fifth year**: *"stories" of Greece and Rome*
**Sixth year**: *"stories" of the Middle Ages*
**Seventh year**: *history from 1492 to 1789*
**Eighth year**: *U.S. history from 1789 to the present.*

The school would also teach mathematics, science, music, carpentry and domestic science, including cooking and sewing. There were only eight grades, but additional grades and a kindergarten would be added in the next several years. The school had no eighth grade until 1936. The very first students were evenly divided between girls and boys.

The two-story school building had two front entrances; the one most often used at that time is now gone. There were eight classrooms, plus rooms for sewing, clay modeling, wood-working, forging and drafting. There was a library on the first floor, and an assembly hall and a gymnasium on the second floor.

On Monday, the children settled into their classrooms and roll was called. Then the teachers went around to each student and adjusted desk and chair for a perfect fit. The orphans, despite the wishes of the school's founder, wore their uniforms that first day, and continued to wear them until 1907. There was an assembly planned for the first day, but the furniture for the assembly hall had not arrived. Otherwise, things went smoothly.

In the fifty years since Isidore Newman had landed in New Orleans, the city's population had doubled, to 300,000. New Orleans was prospering: the so-called American Sector was bustling with commerce and mansion-building. There were very few cars in New Orleans, but there were thirty streetcar lines. On the other side of the canal that ran down the middle of Claiborne Avenue was swamp and forest, frequented by duck hunters. There was a contentious mayor's race underway, pitting Chas F. Buck of the "home rulers" against Martin Behrman, who was criticized for allowing the governor to call the shots in New Orleans. Mr. Behrman won, and went on to rule New Orleans for seventeen years, though not consecutively. No one has beaten this record, and he ruled New Orleans much in the way the Tammany Hall leaders ruled New York — with an iron and corrupt fist. Because of unseasonably warm weather, Louisiana's cotton crops had come in early, and there weren't enough pickers for the harvest. Teddy Roosevelt was about to be elected president.

October 3, 1904 was the first day of school all over town. There were a record-breaking 25,000 children in public schools, and there were more to come: many parents kept their children out of classes until the weather cooled off. Thousands more children began their year in single-sex parochial and private schools, and hundreds of young adults reported to the colleges and universities. Isidore Newman Manual Training School was reported to be the best equipped school in the city, although it may not have had much competition, especially from other private schools. Louise S. McGehee School was not founded until 1912, New Orleans Academy opened in 1910 and Metairie Park Country Day in 1929. The *Times-Democrat* featured the new school in an October 4 article: "Isidore Newman Manual Training School Throws Open its Doors," read the sub-head on a larger story about the first day of school. "Considerable interest centered around the opening of the Isidore Newman Manual Training School. This is the first and only training school in the city." The article went on to point out some of its assets:

> *The comfort and training of the child has been considered even to such points as providing them with individual stoves for their cooking, and shower baths after exercises in the gymnasium . . . . The enrollment at the school was not as heavy as it was hoped it would be. It is believed the purpose of the school is not thoroughly understood yet.*

*The Daily Picayune* also featured the new school in a story. It highlighted the handsome brick and marble edifice, and noted that children of any creed or denomination were welcome. The only other private, non-parochial school mentioned in the story was Sophie Wright's "Home Institute" for girls.

At first, the school was hungry for paying students, and it even reduced tuition to lure neighborhood children. But it didn't take long for Manual not only to fill its seats but to outgrow its building. And as the school became popular in the community, the students of varied backgrounds did just what Isidore Newman and Isaac Leucht had dreamed: they got along.

The school never forgot its benefactor. In 1907, the school held a celebration for Isidore Newman's seventieth birthday. Many things were said that day, about Isidore Newman the man, and Isidore Newman the school. Mr. Addicott said:

> *If we agree that service to our fellow-men is the highest ideal of life, then we must regard Mr. Newman's gifts to education as the highest and noblest form of giving; for it is Mr. Newman's most earnest wish that his school shall develop in its pupils usefulness, integrity and independence.*

Mr. Newman gave a stirring speech, which turned out to be one of his last at the school. "Why all this celebration in my honor?" he said, according to the *Times-Democrat*.

> *I am sufficiently rewarded by my own consciousness of having done my duty, though I appreciate your thanks from the bottom of my heart. I came over to this country a steerage passenger on a sailing vessel. See what blessings God has showered upon me. Could I take all this and give nothing from the benefits I enjoy? For years it has been the desire of my heart to do something for this city and State which have made me what I am. I have my reward in this school . . . . Why, here we have no uniformed orphans, the rich and the poor stand alike. I have one more wish in life and only one, that is to live just a few years more . . . just to see practical results from this school, to see the children trained here started in life, to give them a helping hand, to help them with my advice, to lend them funds, if necessary, to start them in business. I want to see an alumni of this school of which I can be proud.*

Isidore Newman got his wish; he lived long enough to see the first person graduate from his school: Harold S. Weil, in 1908. It was a class of one. Mr. Weil went on to Tulane University, as would so many Newman graduates over the next one hundred years, and then went into his father's business, Weil Brothers. He also was involved in many community groups; he was president of the congregation at Temple Sinai and treasurer of Touro Infirmary.

Mr. Newman also lived to see the first commencement exercises in 1909. Six boys and three girls received their diplomas in the school's assembly hall. They were handed out by Mr. Henson, who had become the school's second principal in 1908. An article in the *Times-Democrat* reported that "the event was so interesting that the audience of the best people of New Orleans overflowed the large hall into the corridors beyond."

Those first graduates were: Lysle Aschaffenberg, Ringgold Brousseau, Lucy Dillard, Sidney Feibleman, Clark Lebermuth, Hennen Legendre, Marguerite Marshall, Lowrie O'Donnell and Kate Vardin. E.B. Craighead, president of Tulane University, spoke, and then invited the graduates to attend Tulane. Apparently, his invitation was all that was needed for admission. The *Picayune* also reported on the event, calling the school a "flourishing institution."

That summer, Isidore Newman went to visit family in upstate New York. He returned very ill, suffering from liver problems. He died at home on November 30, 1909, with his family at his bedside. Later that same day, black crepe was pinned to the door of the New Orleans Stock Exchange. Crepe with violets — his favorite — hung from the Newman banking house on Carondelet Street. Hundreds of telegrams from all over the country arrived at his home that day. He was hailed as one of the greatest financiers of the South. The funeral was at his home on December 1.

Isidore Newman's children and his wife continued to give gifts to the school, including money, land, a cafeteria and gym equipment. His seven surviving children had twenty-one children, and many of them, their children, and their children's children have attended Newman. Two Newmans have served on the board — Isidore Newman II, and Herman Kohlmeyer Jr., a great-grandson, who served for almost thirty years and was the chairman from 1983 to 1986.

An old tradition, done away with many years ago, was to have a Newman descendant lay a wreath under the founder's portrait on Founder's Day. This was an honor not always cherished by Mr. Newman's descendants. "It was absolutely humiliating," said Jane Newman '55, a great-grandchild of Mr. Newman. "There was Hermie, then his sister, Marie, and then my sister Ellen, then I got stuck with it. All my classmates thought I was somebody special, which I never thought."

But Founder's Day remains one of the most special days of the school year. It is one of the few times when everyone at the school is together in one place, and it has become an occasion to honor teachers, both for years of service and for excellence.

In 1990, 104 descendants of Isidore Newman gathered at the school for a reunion.

In 2003, there were four great-great-great grandchildren of Isidore Newman attending his school.

ABOVE: *Detail, mural by Tony Green. Children in a classroom in the days of manual training.*
LEFT: *Mr. Newman's seventieth birthday. One of Mr. Newman's grandsons is peeking out from the flowers.*

# The Jewish Orphans' Home

WHEN NEWMAN OPENED IN 1904, the Jewish Orphans' Home, then almost fifty years old, housed about 130 children within its imposing walls. The Home, at St. Charles and Jefferson avenues, where the Jewish Community Center is today, was enormous: it was a stone square several stories tall built around an interior courtyard. Inside it was dark and, to some, slightly spooky. Out back was a large yard with enough room for team sports.

Opened in 1856 on Chippewa Street, the Home originally housed Jewish orphans and widows left destitute or alone by the 1853 yellow fever epidemic. In 1875, the Home began accepting children from the seven-state region of B'nai B'rith Number 7, and in turn the regional Jewish organization helped support the New Orleans Association for the Relief of Jewish Widows and Orphans, the Home's umbrella agency. In the 1880s, after more epidemics and the Civil War, the Association for the Relief of Jewish Widows and Orphans raised money for the new, larger home at St. Charles Avenue. The widows and orphans moved there in 1887. A few years later, the association moved the widows out. The most children the Home ever had was 171 in 1913, but the numbers dwindled dramatically in the twentieth century; by 1946, when the Home stopped housing children, there was just a handful in residence.

The Honorable Louis Hano Yarrut '13 lived in the Home from 1896 to 1909:

"During my first years of residence in the Home, the children were regimented," he recalled in *A Century of Progress*, a booklet commemorating the centennial anniversary of the Home. "In military fashion we marched to meals and sat at long

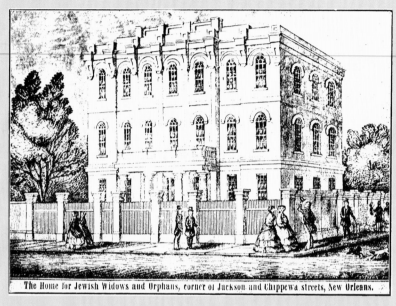

The Home for Jewish Widows and Orphans, corner of Jackson and Chippewa streets, New Orleans.

*A drawing of the first home for Jewish orphans, which opened at the corner of Chippewa Street and Jackson Avenue in 1856.*

tables; we marched to and from school. We marched to every undertaking. We slept in long dormitories with the cots lined up in endless array."

Most of the children had at least one parent, but usually it was a mother or father who had to work or was strapped financially. The "Home kids," as they were known at Newman, wore uniforms when they first began attending their new school, but after a few years, the rule changed and they were allowed to wear regular clothes. Other institutional trappings began to disappear as well. In 1909, the new Home superintendent, Chester J. Teller, dubbed himself "mayor" of the Home's "Golden City," and he divided the children into "families" overseen by Big Sisters and Big Brothers. In 1922, Superintendent Leon

Volmer did away with the long, institutional dining tables and tried even harder to make the children's life there homier. In 1924, the name changed from the Jewish Orphans' Home to Jewish Children's Home, because so many residents had a mother or a father. For the remainder of its history, the Home was nothing like the stereotypical orphanage.

"The Home was actually a home," said Jennie Ogden Schneider '51, who, with her twin sister, Sara, moved there in 1941 when they were eight years old. Their mother, who was single, signed on to be an Army nurse during World War II. "It was the best thing that could have happened to us," Mrs. Schneider said.

The children were given an allowance and allowed to shop downtown for clothes and other necessities. The Home did away with in-house clubs; if children wished to join a scout troop or a team, they could join one in the community. Small, cozy rooms replaced the huge dormitories. And there was help from neighborhood families, who would have the children over for dinner or take them to the movies. Someone in the community set up a dowry fund for the girls, to give them money when they married.

In 1929, Harry L. Ginsburg, affectionately known as "Uncle Harry" by the children, took over as superintendent. In 1938, on the Home's eighty-third anniversary, there was an article in the Sunday *Item-Tribune*: "New Orleans institution is ranked high throughout the nation as a model of its kind; no regimentation, children grow up in informal home-like atmosphere," the subhead read. "Mr. Ginsburg is 'Uncle Harry' and foster father to the children," the article said. "And he feels a deep sense of pride in his 'kids,' and in their growth and development."

Inge Elsas, a supervisor for the girls at the Home from 1940 to 1946, said Mr. Ginsburg provided a personal, parental touch. "He was wonderful — very advanced," she said. "I would go to Newman to be there for PTA meetings and other meetings, because my children had no parents. I was their mom. And we would have cake and ice cream for each child's birthday. I also helped decorate each child's room."

Carol Hart '43 was placed in the Home after his father died, leaving his mother with four boys. They had been living in Jefferson, Texas, with Mr. Hart's grandmother and aunts, but his mother didn't want her children growing up in a small Texas town in a house full of older ladies.

"She left Jefferson in 1926 and took a train to New Orleans," Mr. Hart said. She'd heard about the Home, and she placed her three youngest boys there. Mr. Hart lived there from 1926 until 1942, when he moved in with his mother in her apartment, after his three older brothers left to fight in World War II.

"It was the finest child care institution," Mr. Hart said of

*Kindergarten at the Jewish Orphans' Home on St. Charles Avenue (From* The Story of the Jewish Orphans' Home.*)*

the Home. He remembers living in a small room with one of his brothers, and eating meals at tables that sat six or eight children.

Mrs. Schneider remembers all the treasures on the Home's grounds. There was a large goldfish pond in the courtyard, and athletic equipment and a jungle gym in the huge yard. The children used to roller skate around and around the cement sidewalk under the porches. She remembers the thrill of taking the streetcar, all by themselves, for shopping trips to Canal Street.

Mrs. Schneider's fondest memories are from her summers at the beach. In 1919, the Jewish Federation opened a camp in Bay St. Louis, Mississippi, and Home children would spend many weeks there each summer. Mrs. Schneider remembers the excitement of taking the train and staying in a rambling, wooden, Victorian home facing the bay. There was fishing, crabbing, Fourth of July picnics and hikes into town to go to the movies or the dime store. The children wrote and acted out skits. She remembers writing and acting out skits in a pavilion and telling ghost stories at night.

*Sarah Ogden Sweet '51 and Jennie Ogden Schneider '51, twin sisters who lived at the Home.*

Most Home kids remember fitting right in at Newman, and many Newman alumni who did not grow up at the Home say they have similar memories. Moise Steeg '32 said he and his classmates made a special effort to befriend the Home kids. Joseph Bihari '43, who lived in the Home, said he knew he was with the "elite of New Orleans" at school, but it was never an

issue. "Everybody was so nice," he said. And, he added with a smile, "The Home kids were the best students and the best athletes."

"I can still honestly say those were the happiest years of my life," said Pat Samuels '42, who lived at the Home with two siblings. He was a basketball star at Newman who went to Rice University with an athletic scholarship, and flew fifty-eight missions during World War II.

There were Newman events at the Home, such as plays and recitals, and some clubs even held their regular meetings there. Herman Kohlmeyer Jr. '49 remembers his fraternity met there every Sunday night.

Other Newman children liked to visit the Home for games and sleepovers. "It was such a treat," said Elise Silverman Blumenfeld '48, who used to spend the night there. "It was a great big place. I sort of envied them — they had all these children their own age to play with."

There were, of course, some differences between the Home kids and the rest of the student body. Carol Hart remembers walking back to the Home for lunch every day — unless it was raining.

"When it rained, we couldn't do that," he said. "So the Home prepared individual lunches and sent them over to the school office. Over the loudspeaker system would come the announcement that lunch for the Home kids was in the office. Some kids were embarrassed."

Still, Mr. Hart and others felt fortunate to attend school with children from private homes. "For fourteen years, I was side by side with students who were in the upper echelons of New Orleans society," Mr. Hart said. "I am proud of and grateful for everything that the Jewish community has afforded me when my family could not."

Lillian Hoftsetter Pulitzer, who moved to the Home in the twenties when she was five years old because her mother had died and her father worked on ships, has a similar memory. She knew she was different, but she didn't feel ostracized.

"I remember the rich kids with their fancy lunches and their cashmere sweaters," Mrs. Pulitzer said. "I remember I saw one of the rich kids — that was how I thought of all the other kids, as the rich kids — and he had an artichoke, and I'd never seen one. I was enchanted. I was proud to go to Newman. It had prestige. It gave me delusions of grandeur that I've never recovered from. But I didn't harbor any jealousy. It was a nice exposure."

Mrs. Schneider said she got the chance to do things that normally would have been difficult for a first-generation American, the daughter of a single mom from Latvia. She remembers being in a sorority and going to dances and society parties.

*Dining room (From* The Story of the Jewish Orphans' Home.*)*

"Some of my friends on occasions thought I should 'hush-hush' the fact that I was once a resident of the Home," wrote Judge Yarrut in *A Century of Progress*. "My reply has always been that I would be an ingrate to do so. If I have accomplished anything, it is my duty to make acknowledgement and help the Home, so that future children in similar circumstances may have help."

Mr. Ginsburg died in 1946, the same year the Home stopped taking in children. There were only thirty-one children left in a building made for 150. Thanks to federal programs created in the 1930s, orphanages were disappearing nationwide. In addition, the Home lost its financial commitment from B'nai B'rith. Those children still in need of a place to live were sent to a home in Cleveland, Ohio. Others were sent back to their parents.

Although both Newman and Christian Brothers wanted to buy the property at 5342 St. Charles Avenue, the Home instead leased it, free of charge, to the Jewish Federation, so it could be used as a community center. The "Home" became a multi-service agency for children in a seven-state region called the Jewish Children's Regional Service. The agency eventually sold the building, for $50,000, to the Jewish Community Center.

In its ninety-year history, the Home housed, clothed, fed and educated 2,000 children.

*Science lab at Isidore Newman Manual Training School in the late 1920s.*

# CHAPTER THREE

# Head and Heart, Hand and Body

*The policy of the Isidore Newman Manual Training School is not merely to teach boys and girls how to make beautiful and useful articles of wood and iron, and copper and brass, but to industrialize the entire process of instruction in school life.*

HEADMASTER CLARENCE C. HENSON, *1910*

EWMAN, OR RATHER, MANUAL, in the first decades was an intimate, neighborhood school with simple charms. Children walked or rode bikes or roller-skated to 1831 Peters Avenue, sloshing through the mud of unpaved side streets. There were fields out back, as well as the cemetery, then overgrown and weedy. "We'd be taken out there as a sort of field trip, looking at weeds, plants, bugs," recalled Karlem Reiss '29. "We enjoyed that immensely."

In the very first years, the girls wore their hair in soft piles or pinned with lush satin ribbons; older girls wore long dresses and hats. The boys endured high, stiff collars and wore short pants until they were about fifteen. They all bought their shoes at Imperial Shoe Store on Canal Street. There was no cafeteria, so children brought their lunch from home. Once the football team formed, the boys practiced in a field where the Saratoga building stands today. Edward Newton "Buddy" Kearny Jr. '18 remembers one of the first football fight songs:

> *Manual will shine tonight!*
> *Manual will shine!*
> *Manual will shine tonight!*

There were sneaky trips to corner stores — forbidden without permission from one's par-

LEFT: *Class of 1923.*

*Faculty, 1928–29.*

E. NEWTON KEARNEY, JR.
President Senior Class.

*LEFT: Edward Newton "Buddy" Kearny Jr. '18 in his graduation portrait in the* Pioneer. *RIGHT: Mr. Kearny at his one-hundredth birthday celebration in 2000 with members of the Newman Student Executive Committee. Photo by Kate Elkins.*

ents. At parties, dances included the waltz and the two-step, and, Mr. Kearny said, "something with a French name where you bow to each other." In classes, students studied German, ancient history and math, and they learned to sew and cook and make wonderful, grown-up things such as tables and lamps. They read and memorized still-popular classics — *Alice in Wonderland, The Legend of Sleepy Hollow* — and Victorian literature, such as *Sesame and Lilies* by John Ruskin.

It wasn't unheard of to see a farmer and his cow crossing Peters Avenue. Fruit and vegetable vendors rode by in mule-drawn carts, as did the lady with her lilting call: "BLAAACK-BERRIES!" The Roman Candy man was there, selling his long sticks of pink confection — although one has to wonder if his cart was as cockeyed and rickety then as it is today.

Once Manual had added high school grades and a kinder-garten, it became popular in the Uptown community it inhab-ited. In quickly increasing numbers, children from middle- and upper-class homes were attending Manual. "My mom was sent there because it was where the nice children went," said Catherine Cahn Kahn '48, daughter of Bertha Jacobson Cahn '23. "It immediately got to be the place to go, socially."

By 1909, Manual had far more children from private homes than from the Jewish Orphans' Home. Enrollment grew rapidly: there were 340 students enrolled for the school year 1909–1910. Of the eighty-nine in the high school, only four-teen came from the Home.

TOP: *The school's vegetable garden in 1909. The property for the garden was donated by Mr. Newman.* BOTTOM: *Exhibit of items made in shop class, 1929.*

In 1909, the Valmont Building was added and the elementary grades moved there. The Saratoga Building was added in 1917 for arts and sciences, and Manual's first freestanding gymnasium was built in 1918. After this early expansion, the school would add no more buildings until 1947.

Tuition for children who were not from the Home ranged from $50 for kindergarten to $100 for high school. The rates did not go up until 1920. There was no entrance exam.

For at least two decades, the school turned out not only well-educated young adults, but also impressive handicrafts. Educators and general observers visited constantly to watch manual training in action.

"Everybody acknowledges the value and importance of industrial training for the young, and there is widespread sentiment in favor of introducing this feature into the public schools of New Orleans," said a 1911 article in the *Times-Democrat*.

Things made in woodworking classes would make a modern-day shop teacher blush with shame. High school boys, working in oak and mahogany, crafted corner cabinets, Mission-style chairs, settees, porch swings and entire dining room sets. They learned mechanical drawing and would draft things before making them. They fashioned lanterns and candlesticks out of hammered copper and iron. The girls sewed their own graduation dresses, threw pots and made luncheons for the football team. Girls as young as five years old were making tiny pillows and mattresses for handmade dollhouses. A few girls even learned woodworking and made furniture; there is no evidence any boys took sewing or cooking.

"I made a wonderful pair of mahogany candlesticks," said Sydney Besthoff III, who attended Newman from 1932 to 1942 and was chairman of the Board of Governors from 1977

to 1980. "I made them on a lathe, and I cut my hands to pieces."

Buddy Kearny remembers woodworking and gardening: "I grew the biggest cabbage one year!" he said. When he was 102, he still had two letter boxes he had made at Manual, each stained a very dark brown and smoothed by years of use. "We'd polish things about 10 or 12 times," he said.

Under the direction of Zelia C. Christian, first a science and nature study teacher and later the assistant principal, the girls grew flowers and the boys grew vegetables in a large garden on school grounds. The property had been donated by Mr. and Mrs. Isidore Newman on Founder's Day, 1909, and was bounded by South Franklin, Valmont, Saratoga and Dufossat streets. Initially, the boys kept the produce, but it was discovered they were eating "vast quantities of raw vegetables" — apparently a bad thing — so each boy was then told to sell the things he grew in his ten-foot square plot. He could keep twenty-five percent of what he earned. A middleman was appointed from each grade to facilitate sales to parents and people around the neighborhood.

Often, manual training reinforced lessons learned in academic classes. For example, a child studying Greek and Roman history might then create Doric, Ionic and Corinthian columns in bas-relief during pottery class.

"It was all delightful play," the *Times-Democrat* reported. "Every child has a passion for making things. A school like this only gratifies that passion, and leads the making into orderly lines."

Beginning the first year, the school held an annual exhibit of the children's work. "Seldom, if ever, has a finer exhibit been witnessed," *The Daily States* gushed in 1909.

Of course, furniture styles are a matter of taste. Marjorie

Isaacs Kullman '31 said there was furniture in her grand-mother's house that her uncle had made at Manual.

"It was leather-upholstered wood, and it wasn't very pretty," she recalled. "It was boxy-looking. When I was punished, I had to sit in a stool that was part of that set."

Mrs. Kullman was no kinder about her own abilities:

"I sewed only one thing. I made a dress, and it was sewn completely by hand. I was very proud of myself. A friend's mother saw me and started laughing. She said I looked like a sausage in a sausage skin.

"I never sewed again."

Lillian Hofstetter Pulitzer, who was at Manual for about ten years in the 1920s and 1930s, has a fonder memory of her sewing class. "I made an outfit — a white pique dress and jacket that I won a prize for," she said. "It was stunning. It had a cowl neck."

In the summer of 1906, the Manual boys took their talents to the woods. Mr. Addicott chaperoned a field trip to Saluda, North Carolina, where the boys did amazingly resourceful things such as making tennis courts out of crumbled granite, making wooden floors and even cabinets for their canvas tents, and creating a shower-bath. Andrée Keil Moss '55 said her father, who was in one of the first classes at Manual, took a field trip to see the Panama Canal — an object lesson in engineering.

"Manual" began evolving into "Newman" long before the name of the school changed in 1931. Clarence Henson, principal of Newman for much of the first fifty years, thought highly of manual training, but he was a practical man. As early as 1910, most graduates were going to college, so the curriculum needed to focus more on college preparatory work. The *Pioneer*, the student magazine, ran an ad every month saying Manual

students would be accepted without examination to several prestigious colleges and universities, including Newcomb College, Tulane University, Louisiana State University, Cornell University, University of Michigan, University of Virginia, University of the South and Smith College. The list would change through the years but the prestige level remained the same.

By the 1920s, the Jewish Orphans' Home was evaluating its charges before they went to high school to determine whether they should continue at Manual in hopes of going to college or instead pursue a more job-oriented course of study at one of the new vocational schools that had opened in New Orleans. "I chose to leave Newman my freshman year and I went to Joseph Kohn," said Mrs. Pulitzer, who lived in the Home. "I took shorthand, typing, and bookkeeping. When I was sixteen, I went to work for an attorney." By 1937, only fifty-two children from the Home attended Newman, compared with 429 children from private homes.

Clarence Henson became principal when Mr. Addicott resigned in 1908 to return to his native California. Mr. Henson had resigned from Manual himself the year before to be superintendent of the Rapides Parish schools in central Louisiana. When Mr. Addicott announced he was leaving, Manual's leaders asked Mr. Henson to return. He would leave once more, in 1917, but when he returned in 1919, it would be for the remainder of his career.

Mr. Henson was a born educator. "I never had any doubt from the beginning, as to what I was going to do with my life," he once said. "I knew always that I would be a teacher."

Clarence Cherrington Henson was born January 8, 1875, on a farm in Jackson County, Ohio. He attended a one-room school house where, he once said, "We were packed in like sar-

*An early Latin class at Manual.*

for his master's degree at Columbia, which he received in 1904.

That same year, Mr. Henson's Columbia classmate, James Addicott, told him he had accepted a position as principal of a new manual training school in New Orleans. Mr. Henson had never been to New Orleans, but Mr. Addicott had, and he painted a tempting picture of the city. Most appealing to Mr. Henson was his description of the St. Charles Avenue streetcar, which his friend said ran through grass and flowers instead of on paved streets. When he arrived, he wound up getting another treat: he rode in one of the first automobiles in New Orleans, belonging to Isidore Newman.

For four years, Mr. Henson, a trim, tidy man of medium height with ruddy skin and wire-framed glasses perched on a strong nose, served as vice-principal and taught history. During that time, he married Nell Blanche Wilson, who was as petite and delicate as he was. They would have a son, Clarence "Chick" Crawford Henson, a large, rugged boy who would attend Newman and later coach and teach gym at his father's school. They lived most of their lives at 1122 Short Street.

Mr. Henson's two departures from Manual suggest he was conflicted about where he could best serve. He felt drawn to the important work of leading a large, public education system, but in the end, Manual always called him back.

He was a formal and strict leader, known for dragging mis-behaving students into his office by their ears. "He was keeping

dines in a can." Studious, energetic and athletic, his only admitted childhood misdemeanor was setting his family's house on fire when he was five years old. He had a typical rural upbringing spent jumping fences, riding horses, playing baseball and studying. He particularly liked geography. At sixteen, he took the exams for a teacher's certificate and a year later, became a teacher in his home state. He was paid $33 a month, and in three years, he saved enough to pay his tuition at a college preparatory school and then at Ohio University in Athens, Ohio. After college, he became principal of Athens High School, where he stayed for three years. He left Ohio to study hold of everything," says Karlem Reiss '29. "Not to the point of being a dictator, but just as being a friend who ran a tight ship."

He allowed the kids to be kids, but also knew when to draw the line. In 1922, upperclassmen were having a little too much fun making the "freshies" wear green and white caps all fall. The *Pioneer* said hazing freshmen produced "dignified" seniors; but Mr. Henson, after tolerating the practice for some time, ended it when "a little too much force was used in 'disciplining' the freshmen."

"He was a very stern, austere man," said Herman Kohlmeyer Jr. '49. "He was the last guy that ever thought about nurturing anybody. But he imbued the school with excellence."

He actively promoted school spirit and involvement in school activities; in 1923, he came up with a slogan to encourage all children to join an athletic team: "Every boy and girl in a game."

He did not believe in wasting anything, especially one's education. Educated people have a duty to society, he said, time and again. He was a passionate defender of democracy, equality and freedom, and he drummed into his students that wealth was meaningless without good character.

A 1922–23 Manual brochure shows Mr. Henson's influence on the school: it says Manual "attempts to train boys and girls who will become interested in the world around them." It teaches that "wealth is no evidence of one's worth, that the favored must make a return in proportion to their advantages, and that the only respectable aristocracy is an aristocracy of honorable achievement and personal decency."

Mr. Henson carefully studied new teaching theories, experimenting with them but keeping only what worked. In the high school, he tried the Dalton plan, which taught social responsibility and emphasized instruction tailored to the individual. The primary classes tested the Winnetka system, which also stressed individualism but did away with traditional grading. Miss Christian and the teachers of the first, second and third grades even went to Winnetka, Illinois, to study the method. Mr. Henson and the teachers would use pieces of each of these methods, but took none in its entirety.

Mr. Henson was widely regarded as one of the South's top educators, and taught for many years at Tulane's summer school. In 1936, Mr. Henson was appointed by Governor James A. Noe to the state Board of Education. An editorial in *The New Orleans Item* said Mr. Henson was "a leader in secondary education" and that he had made Newman "one of the most outstanding private institutions in the South."

Mr. Henson had strong opinions and fervent beliefs. Here's a sampling of his words:

> *Do the boys and girls who are about to leave us realize that they belong to a picked class of young people, a class from which the leaders and directors of public affairs are generally chosen?*

> *In this amusement-loving age in which we live there are so many alluring invitations to pleasure-seeking that many yield to the temptation to forget industry and seek pleasure. In some places, with some people, it is fashionable to sneer at the serious questions of life . . . . We must never forget that the world does not owe us a living. On the contrary, we owe the world a debt which it will be difficult to pay. We fail to make good our place in the world unless we add something to the commonwealth, become producers as well as consumers; producers in things material, likewise producers in things of the mind.*

*Class of 1928.*

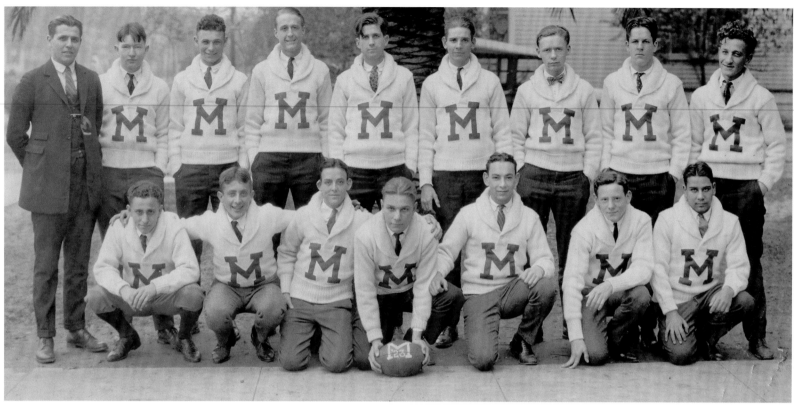

*The 1923 Greenies.*

We may be far more widely educated than our fathers were, but I strongly suspect that we are not as deeply educated as they were.

There are boys and girls who have no business in college. Some because they simply do not have the mental capacity for the college courses. Some because they see in college nothing but a chance to make a team or make a frat; or what they consider the present and subsequent social advantages of being a college man or a college woman.

College is worth almost any sacrifice to the boy or girl who has a definite purpose of fitting themselves for life's serious work by a college foundation.

The most important thing to be considered in the pursuit of one's studies is this: am I learning how to use my mind effectively? The mind is a tool. One has to learn how to use it. That is what studies are for . . . . Boys and girls who learn how to use their minds will become the leaders of their day and generation, while those who fail to learn how to use their minds are destined to be followers during all the days of their life.

*Students in 1923 dressed up for a "circus" party.*

In the 1910s, the school teemed with hundreds of students and activity. There was a full-fledged sports program with Claude "Monk" Simons Sr. as the coach. The boys played football and basketball; the girls played basketball at school but not with other teams. In fact, games between Newman girls and other schools were not permitted. Boy and girl athletes who "lettered" donned thick, woolly sweaters emblazoned with an "M" for Manual.

The school year ran from the first Monday in October until the second Friday in June and there were two terms. Kindergarteners were in school from 9 in the morning until noon, first and second graders until 12:30 P.M., third through seventh graders until 2:50 P.M. and high-schoolers until 3:30 P.M.

Students had no homework until fifth grade, when they were expected to do one hour of homework a day. High school students had two hours of homework a day. Reports were sent home once a month. Any student who scored 90 percent or more in a class didn't have to take the final exam.

In gym class, the children practiced "Swedish free standing exercises simplified." "Round shoulders, drooping head, and flat chests are the leading defects in many high school pupils," according to a 1913 school handbook. "The exercises given aim to correct such defects and improve the condition of vital organs." Kindergarteners spent as much time as possible outside, because it was thought children needed open air to develop normally.

There was a German club, drama club, French club, debating club and a student body organization. The *Pioneer,* a school magazine begun in 1911, came out nine times a year, with the final issue, the "senior number," serving as a precursor to the yearbook of later years. The debate club argued timely subjects such as: "Resolved: That foreign immigration to the United States be further restricted by the imposition of an educational test." Senior essays were sometimes strangely timeless: "The Influence of the South on the Nation," and "How to Reduce the High Cost of Living" were 1913 essays.

There were strict rules regarding infectious diseases; even though the last outbreak of yellow fever was in 1905, many other diseases, including influenza, were killers. If someone in a student's home was sick with an infectious disease, that child might not be allowed at school until a health official deemed the household no longer infectious. A dance was cancelled in 1917 because of a measles outbreak.

Beginning in 1907, there was an annual Founder's Day program; it was four hours long, followed by an early dismissal.

The fall of 1917 was a hard one for Manual — and the nation. The United States had entered World War I in April, and at Manual, Mr. Henson was gone, presumably for good. In his place came two principals who each stayed one year. The first was C.C. Hayden, who trained at Peabody Institute in Nashville. A *Pioneer* article described him: "He is kind and stern, just as the occasion demands itself . . . . He is about the average height, weighing about 135 pounds, wears glasses, has some gray hairs, and green eyes, and presents a neat and business-like appearance."

Mr. Hayden had trouble filling the shoes of his predecessor. "The students were in a measure demoralized by the fact that a new principal was to take the place of OUR Mr. Henson," the *Pioneer* reported. He lasted one year.

In 1918, John W. Curtis — a Texan with experience in vocational and manual training schools — tried his hand at leading Manual, but after one year, school officials did not ask him back. The school went to Mr. Henson and offered him a

*Class of 1936 in Elementary School.*

generous salary, $6,000, and a promise that the school board wanted to make Manual the best prep school in the South. In his letter of resignation to the Rapides Parish school board, Mr. Henson said it was an offer he couldn't refuse. Zelia C. Christian, who had been teaching science, became his assistant principal.

By December, 1917, seventy-eight Manual graduates were in the armed forces. At school, the students organized to send the men blankets, sweaters and helmets, "in short anything that will give the soldier comfort and remind him that he is in the thoughts of those at home," the *Pioneer* said. Girls from the Jewish Orphans' Home knitted sweaters. All students were urged in the *Pioneer* to "lick up your plate and help lick the Kaiser." Manual stopped teaching German and did away with the German club.

By the spring of 1918, 103 Manual men were at war. In a show of patriotism, the class of 1918 gave the school an American flag in a ceremony on the front steps of the Jefferson Building.

After the war, the school enjoyed a surge in activity and school spirit. The garden, fallow for years, was thriving once again. Thanks to a gift from Isidore Newman's children, the school set up its first cafeteria in 1920. New teachers, beloved legends who would stay for decades, arrived that year, including Eugenia Poole, Pauline Mizzi, G. Campbell Cooksey and Florence Kerwin.

Karlem Reiss, who attended Manual from 1924 to 1929, said manual training at that time was more of an elective than a central part of the curriculum: "I took manual training one semester and mechanical drawing one semester, and I was a miserable flop at both. I never have been able to work with my hands."

Tuition in the late 1920s ranged from $75 to $240. There was a $5 fee for general science; the athletic fee was $5 for boys, $3 for girls. Enrollment was over 600, although it would drop dramatically during the Depression. In fact, many private schools nationwide closed in the 1930s because of a lack of students.

In 1922, at the request of the senior class, Mr. Cooksey staged an operetta, *The Maid and the Middy* by G.L. Tracy, at the Jewish Orphans' Home. The operetta became a tradition that would last for decades.

There were "wireless concerts" in the Physics classroom; students got a lesson in static one night when rain interfered with the reception. In 1925, Mr. Henson helped resurrect the student government. The new one had eighteen students — three boys and three girls from each of the three upper classes. They held their first meeting on January 23, 1925, with the girls in one room and the boys in another.

On weekends, there were fraternity and sorority activities, and girls hosted parties with themes such as "tacky," "circus" and "Greenwich Village." But there was little or no drinking or other teenage misbehaving.

Moise Steeg '32 said it was a huge treat just to eat a meal out: "One of my classmates had a car — I can still see it — and two or three of us would get together and we'd go to the K&B and we'd get a milkshake and a sandwich for 25 cents. Now that was a big deal. I was all of fifteen years old."

In 1930, when Manual celebrated its twenty-fifth anniversary, more than 500 students had graduated; eighty percent of them had gone on to college. And Manual was enjoying many successes. Mr. Henson called a special assembly on November 7 because Manual won its first football league championship. It would win again in 1931 and 1932. Manual's football team was called the "Greenies" even then, or sometimes the "Green Wave," just like Tulane's.

Thanks to Walter Allee, the science teacher, Manual students routinely won the most prizes of any Louisiana school in a national chemical essay contest given by the American Chemical Society. One year, a Manual girl placed first in the nation and received a four-year scholarship to Wellesley College. In 1930, Manual won more prizes than any school in the country. There were other honors: for decades, Manual was the only place in New Orleans to take the College Entrance Examination Boards, required for entry at most Eastern colleges, and in 1930, it became the first school in the state to be accredited by the Southern Association of Colleges and Secondary Schools.

Mr. Henson looked back on the school's first twenty-five years in a speech on Founder's Day:

> *How vividly do I recall the late afternoons in the fall and spring of the first two years of this school when the principal, James Edwin Addicott, and I would walk up to Audubon Park, and tramping through the park, we would discuss and dream about the kind of school we wanted to see established here in New Orleans as a beacon light in our community. We wanted a kindergarten department; we wanted a complete elementary school department, and we wanted a complete high school, preparing boys and girls to go on with their studies in college. You see we were almost bubbling with enthusiasm for the new ideas which agitated us as we were just fresh from Teachers College of Columbia University, a veritable clearing house for ideas on education . . . . Well, ladies and gentlemen, that dream of ours has literally come true. For I have seen the acquisition of grounds, the addition of buildings, an increase in the student body of 500 percent, and an increase in the teaching staff of more than 300 percent, until today we have a complete school plant . . .*

Manual training, all but forgotten around the country, needed to be phased out at Manual. Mr. Henson said in a report to the Parent-Teacher Association in May 1930, "We propose in the future to concentrate our efforts on general education, not attempting to do both general education and vocational education. We interpret the function of a school such as ours to be that of training — training to read, training to think, training to study, training in citizenship, and training in character building."

In the spring of 1931, the graduating class left Newman, not Manual. The change was not insignificant; students wrote passionate essays for and against the name change. One student called the name Manual "old-fashioned and out-of-date," while another said that "to change the name now would be to destroy its fine tradition."

Isidore Cohn Jr. '38, the 2002–2003 Distinguished Alumnus, remembers the school's name changing about the same time Peters Avenue became Jefferson Avenue. "It was confusing to all of us," he said. "We were going to a school that wasn't what it was, and it wasn't on the street where it was."

An expanded arts and crafts department replaced manual training. In 1938, the Education Committee of the Home — which governed the school until 1946 — discontinued courses in cooking and sewing, dealing the final blow to manual training. The modern era at Newman had begun.

# The Pioneer:
## Louisiana's Oldest Student Literary Magazine

### GRADUATION SONG
#### (To the tune of Ciribiribin)

In the School of Manual Training
There've been classes sweet and dear
Those that linger in the mem'ry
And whose mem'ries always cheer,
But the class which is the brightest,
There is magic in its name,
It is known throughout the country,
It's the class of the greatest fame,
This class so bright,
With it's shining lights,
‖ Is the class for me, ‖ for me, for me,
Nineteen, nineteen, nineteen.

#### CHORUS

Nineteen is what I mean,
For it's the best class ever seen,
Nineteen forever tells of days so perfect and serene,
Nineteen our love for you
Is burning ever bright and true
Nineteen, nineteen,
The best class ever seen.

EVELYN KAHN LEVY

*An early song about the school composed by Evelyn Kahn Levy '19.*

THE *PIONEER*, Newman's literary magazine since 1911, is the oldest continuously published school magazine in Louisiana. Initially the only school publication, it was the place for news, gossip, essays, announcements, poems and short stories. It was even the yearbook: the June issue was called the "senior number" and had features on each graduate. The *Pioneer*, which came out nine times a year, at first was printed by the Tulane Press; for a period in the 1920s and 1930s, it was printed at Steeg Printing, owned by the father of Moise Steeg '32. Students made wood and linoleum cuts in art class to illustrate the *Pioneer*. The covers ranged from primitive to beautiful, and often were timely: in June, 1944, the cover depicted a student exchanging his diploma for a rifle. Others marked the seasons with pictures of Santa or Mardi Gras maskers. Sometimes the whole issue would be themed to something like the Aztecs, or Cajuns.

In the early years, there was a feature called the "Exchange," in which *Pioneer* editors critiqued magazines from schools around the country, and they would in turn critique the *Pioneer*. There was a "Jokes" section for decades, with witticisms like:

*Young lady: You say you were on a raft for six weeks and you had nothing to eat but mutton. Where did you get the mutton from?*

*Old Salt: Well, you see, Miss, the sea was very choppy.*

*An early cover of the* Pioneer, *Newman's student magazine, which is the oldest continuously published student magazine in Louisiana.*

In 1930, the *Pioneer* won first place in a national contest sponsored by the Columbia Scholastic Press Association of Columbia University. The proud *Pioneer* staff mounted the telegram announcing the win on a wall, as it came conveniently in time for the annual exhibit.

There were political essays. In 1935, Frederick D. King Jr. '36 asked: "Is war imminent?"

> *Once again the God Mars is rattling the saber in the scabbard and the Four Horsemen of the Apocalypse are galloping over the horizon! Once more the measured tread of marching feet and the roar of guns fill the air. Not since 1914, when Germany hurled her titanic military across the border of Belgium, has the world been so utterly on the brink of the abyss War.*

In 1939, the magazine grew larger and slicker, and in the early years of World War II, perhaps because of some talented students, it was especially witty, and very gossipy. "The Fifth Column" debuted in 1943 as a comedic sendoff to the conspiracy theory about a rogue group terrorizing Europe. It was introduced this way: "When people see the heading of this page, they're going to say, 'Is Newman unpatriotic? Has the *Pioneer* started a column telling what's happening in the sabotage field today?' Put down that F.B.I. badge. We are all writing in fun."

It was a gossip column, with items introduced with "threats" such as, "We burn a village for . . ." or "A Pepsi Cola flavored with arsenic is served to . . ."

When the *Greenie* began publishing in 1954, the *Pioneer* held its own for a while, continuing to print news and gossip. But by the late sixties, it was a pure literary magazine, and began to resemble the *Pioneer* of today.

*A Newman band in 1932.*

# CHAPTER FOUR

# A Golden Era

Eugenia Seavey Shirley '46:

*It was just fun. The whole thing was fun.*

Katherine Talbot Holmquist '46:

*Best years of my life.*

Eugenia: *Me, too. Absolutely.*

Interview with the Author, *2003*

THEY GREW UP DURING the Great Depression, in the shadow of World War II, and in its jubilant yet uncertain aftermath. Newman students of the 1930s and 1940s lived in a time when their parents were preoccupied with monumental national and world events. For the children — for whom hard times meant gas rations, not true hunger — it was a time of suspended reality, like a snow day that never ends. Perhaps school felt like a haven created just for them, where kids could be kids and the harsh realities of the world could be kept at bay for a few precious years. "Those were easy times," said Herman Kohlmeyer Jr. '49. "We had a lot of fun."

"It was before television, before computers," said Andrée Keil Moss '55. "We listened to the radio, and we listened to our parents. And school had a great influence on us."

Carmel Cohen '50, the 1998–1999 Distinguished Alumnus, called it "a magical era:"

> New Orleans at that time was a city where you couldn't get a bad meal, where things were really safe. We had the run of the city for exploration and enjoyment. We could ride horses on the levee at night; we could walk the neutral grounds of St. Charles and Claiborne avenues — at night, as kids, unsupervised.

LEFT: *Class of 1934.*

By the mid-1930s, half a million people called New Orleans home. Robert Maestri, the wealthy and controversial mayor, set the city back on firm financial footing after the Depression. Former Populist governor and U.S. Senator Huey Long was assassinated in 1935, the same year New Orleans was blanketed under an historic inch of snow. Bonnie and Clyde were killed by police in Shreveport in 1934. Banjo Annie was the queen of the French Quarter. Audubon Park opened its swimming pool in 1928. The dry years of Prohibition were over. Television had been invented but radio still ruled — kids listened to *Orphan Annie* while their parents were hooked on *One Man's Family*. It was an era of great movie stars — Judy Garland in *The Wizard of Oz*, James Cagney in *The Public Enemy* and Jean Harlow in *Dinner at Eight*. Amelia Earhart had flown solo across the Atlantic. Adolph Hitler had been appointed chancellor of Germany, and as the decade progressed, all eyes were on Europe as war loomed ever closer.

Isidore Cohn Jr. '38 remembers riding his bike to school when Nashville Avenue was "a wiggling, gravel street," and the old Shakespeare retirement home had cows roaming out back. Willard Marmelzat '35 painted a vivid picture of the early thirties in Uptown New Orleans when he spoke at a 2001 reception honoring him as that year's Distinguished Alumnus:

*Mud! I remember mud, lots of it. The streets between my home and this school were not yet paved. Thank God we boys wore knickerbockers and not long pants; trousers would not have stood the assault. Often, we would steal away in these muddy streets. Sometimes, a few of us would dine out for lunch! Our destination: a mama and papa Italian deli called Giuliano's . . . a fragrant palace of vats of pickled pigs' feet.*

*I remember sounds — not just the many sounds that arose from a close relationship to mud, but more defined ones. Radio was approaching its heyday. Coming out of the houses along the way to school were the voices of the very first news and sportscasters . . .*

*Walking to school, I still remember seeing the red notices on the doors of houses — red marks that meant quarantine. On a happier note were the many bright colors of gumballs in the first-ever gumball machines . . .*

*The boys and girls of my generation will remember fondly an olive-skinned grizzled little fellow we called Roasty-Toasty. He existed somewhere in Bohemia, something in between a busker (street musician), and a beggar. Roasty-Toasty was an organ grinder, with a small, handle-driven concertina, a little, seemingly emaciated monkey on one shoulder, and bags of peanuts for us kids to feed that cooperative, clever simian sidekick . . . Roasty-Toasty wore, even as summer approached, seemingly endless layers of silken clothing — reds, yellows and greens . . .*

Newman School, then still owned by the Jewish Orphans' Home, was valued at $250,000 in the thirties. It remained a neighborhood school where classmates knew each other's mothers and fathers, their older and younger siblings. Teachers, especially the Lower School teachers, were often matronly women with their hair pulled back in buns. The children adored them, and the teachers revered their boss, Mr. Henson. Many Newman alumni remember being in kindergarten for two years

*RIGHT: An early track practice.*

— it may have been an option offered to Depression and war era mothers, to give them a place to park a younger child while they went to work.

By the early thirties, the magical "Greentrees" playground and the tennis courts where Francis Soyka reigned for generations had been built on plots of land recently acquired by the school. Greentrees has such a mystique about it that alumni debate where it was, even though there's a plaque on campus placing it near where the bookstore is now.

"Oh, Greentrees," Ellie Woodward von Voorthuyen '43 said with a sigh. "It was wide open, and there were a lot of trees, and we danced around like fairies."

New clubs were always forming in the years leading up to World War II, including the Junior Red Cross, the Spanish club, French club, science club, camera club, a chess and checkers club and a senior debating club. The Green Lizards for boys and the White Daisies for girls promoted school spirit. The Green Lizards even became the athletic teams' names, but only for about a year. An invitation-only club called Tri-G, which stood for Girls Good Government, encouraged school spirit and tried to make students respect the school grounds, and each other.

Students were active in community service, even before World War II. The children found all kinds of ways to help the orphans at St. Elizabeth's Orphans Asylum — a touching fact considering there were still children from the Home attending Newman. They donated Christmas presents and Thanksgiving baskets and performed plays and musical recitals at the asylum.

Music, just as Isidore Newman had hoped, was a major component of life at Newman. And the one thing almost everyone joined was Mr. Cooksey's operetta. "By the time you were a junior, you could croak like a frog but if you showed up

and showed an interest, you were in the chorus," said Cathy Cahn Kahn '48. As many as one hundred children would be on stage during productions of *The Pirates of Penzance, The Mikado,* and *Iolanthe.* Even those with no talent could blend in. "A cousin of mine remained dead drunk and propped up by friends during the finale of *Pirates of Penzance,*" said Mr. Kohlmeyer. And there was plenty of work backstage, creating sets and setting up lights. "I helped backstage, even after I graduated," said Karlem Reiss '29.

G. Campbell Cooksey, a graduate of Vanderbilt University, came to Newman in 1920 from his job as an assistant supervisor of music in Nashville's public schools. After the first operetta was performed in the Home in 1922, Mr. Cooksey staged his productions in the gym for several years. Then, from 1929 to 1937, the performances were held outside in the school's courtyard, on a spring night in the glow of flood lights. The stage curtains were hung on a cable between two buildings. The lighting became an annual project for Walter Allee's physics class. In 1938, the operetta moved to Dixon Hall on Tulane's campus. Wherever it was, it was no small affair: costumes for the operettas came from New York, and local professionals made up the orchestra.

Mr. Cooksey was a formal, reserved man. He was demanding, but no wonder — putting on Gilbert and Sullivan is not easy. He thoroughly studied the productions and worked hard to teach his young actors choreographed scenes ("Fans Up!" read one of the many stage directions in the notes he left to Newman) and British comedic timing.

Carol Graves McCall '58, director of advancement at Newman, remembers him as demanding. She was a cheerleader her senior year, which meant she'd scream her lungs out at Friday night games and come to Monday's rehearsals hoarse.

*RIGHT: George Campbell Cooksey, choral leader and producer of Newman's operettas from 1920–1963.* BELOW: *Cast of* Iolanthe, *1940s.*

*An elementary class in the 1920s.*

*Class of 1935.*

"He was furious," she said. "He said, 'You have to decide what you want to be and what you want to do. If you want to sing, you can't go out on Friday night and scream!'"

Students rehearsed all year, two or three times a week. Chorus rehearsals began in the fall, and Mr. Cooksey selected the leads in January. At the time, Tulane was staging annual productions of Gilbert and Sullivan operettas as well, so the many Newman alumni who went to Tulane often performed the same operettas twice between high school and college. "You can't get anybody who went to Newman at that time who can't sing every song from every Gilbert and Sullivan operetta," said Eve Godchaux Hirsch '44.

In the forties, Newman children even did a third operetta during their academic lifetimes — this one in miniature. Thanks to music teacher Annette Bernard, who enlisted the help of art teacher Angela Devlin, fourth graders began making puppets with papier-mâché heads and staging a pint-sized operetta.

"We did *Hansel and Gretel* that first year," Annette Bernard, now Mrs. Brown, recalled.

> Then we started doing Gilbert and Sullivan — you know, watered down versions! The puppets were so cute, and we had a little bitty stage in the auditorium with long paper panels on either side with holes where the chorus puppets would come in. When we staged H.M.S. Pinafore, *the holes became portholes. I wanted to do* The Mikado *at one time, but it was too soon after World War II.*

David Stone '57 remembered painting the head of his puppet and attaching hair to it. "Gilbert and Sullivan was a little sophisticated for fourth graders but Mrs. Bernard tried to help us understand what it all meant," said Mr. Stone. "The lines were spoken and the solos were sung as a chorus — no one had to sing a solo."

Mrs. Bernard and Miss Devlin also were responsible for the May Pole in Greentrees, and they taught the traditional dances to go with it. "We made kilts out of crepe paper," Mrs. Brown said. "I sat up night after night making those. And the gym teacher taught the kids an Irish jig. It was lots of fun. The kids loved to wiggle around."

Band instructor Alfonse J. Guma was hired in 1942 by Mr. Henson to work part-time, because some parents wanted to have a band at football games. He was hoping he was there to lead a real school band, but it turned out that there wasn't one, he said. He was asked instead to help with a small club that had only six students. The band that had begun when the school first opened — thanks to the instruments donated by the Newmans — had dissolved, regrouped and dissolved again. But the original instruments survived, banged up and gathering dust but still usable, in storage at the Home. Mr. Guma retrieved them and, in his words, "started from scratch."

"I began with the Lower School, and we built our own feeder program," he said. By the early 1950s, there were bands in the Lower, Middle and Upper schools. Mr. Guma, having proved himself indispensable, was hired full-time. He stayed until 1978, when his son, Michael, who is the band leader today, took over. The older Mr. Guma, who was 90 in 2003, still teaches private lessons at Newman.

Mr. Guma remembers when Newman's band marched in Mardi Gras parades; when he describes the long and circuitous route Okeanos used to take, it makes one wonder why the kids didn't drop their instruments and quit halfway through. "That was a meanie," he said.

In 1936, Newman added an eighth grade, a recent addi-

*Band instructor A.J. Guma with girls on French horns in the 1950s.*

tion in schools elsewhere in the country. In the late thirties, old shacks were torn down behind the school to enlarge the back field. And the last of the unpaved streets around school were getting their blacktops.

Ruth Dreyfous, a Newman graduate with a master's degree in child development and guidance from Columbia, arrived in 1938 and created the first guidance program in a private school in New Orleans. She instituted the testing of applicants, and her testing methods became the foundation of the admissions process at other private schools. She also created the gifted reading program at Newman.

During the weekend of November 27, 1941, Newman had its first Homecoming. Weekend activities included the school's first-ever night football game; Newman won against Rugby, 32-2. There was a large bonfire on the back lot and a dance in the gym, which was decked out to look like a football field. A band called the Tulanians provided music, and Evelyn Hodges '43 was crowned queen of the Homecoming Court. The court, all girls, was chosen by the male athletes, and the queen was the girl in whose name the most game tickets were sold. "The dance was declared to be one of the best in years, and it is expected that the homecoming celebration will become an annual fixture," the *Pioneer* reported.

In the early forties, the kids were dancing to Glenn Miller and listening to Bob Hope, *Sky King* and *The Lone Ranger* on the radio. The girls wore patriotic accessories, reversible raincoats and increasingly shorter skirts. There was a "girls only" column in the *Pioneer* that dispensed advice on such vital matters as attracting and keeping a man: "Always look nice, don't talk too much, don't talk only about yourself, and don't boast about the other dates you've had."

Senior year, students with good grades were granted privileges, such as leaving school at lunch. Boys would go to Gambino's and get doberge cake, or have a beer at a nearby bar. Girls would pile in a car and cruise Broadway or Freret Street to stand in front of Tulane's fraternity houses. Newman alumni from this era get a certain twinkle in their eyes when they reminisce about their school days. "Those were the best years — I just adored Newman," said Mary Jane Carter Fenner '51. "There was really a sense of belonging, I think for everybody. It was strict, there were rules, but there was a happy feeling."

Listen to women become girls again as they reminisce. Here, Eve Godchaux Hirsch '44, and Cathy Cahn Kahn '48 talk of their school days:

*Eve: I remember Greentrees. It was a wonderful playground. It had trees and bushes and we used to have Easter egg hunts. And do you remember the orange and green teams we had?*

*Cathy: We played volleyball in the courtyard between Valmont and the front building. In the winter, the girls played basketball. In those days you had to stay on one side or the other. You couldn't run the whole court. That was way too much for girls.*

*Eve: We had these bloomers — they were awful, awful. The worst color orange. And I had thighs, so I didn't need anything puffing out.*

*Cathy: The boys and girls ate separately. You brought your lunch and you never ate in the cafeteria. It was uncool.*

*Eve: Although you could get rice and gravy for seven cents. I loved rice and gravy.*

*Girls from the class of 1942.*

*Cathy: You got your lunch out of your locker and you and your five best friends . . .*

*Eve: It was an unwritten law — you sat on the neutral ground under a palm tree. That was our spot.*

*Cathy: There was no uniform, but there WAS a uniform. We wore brown loafers and white bobby socks and a skirt that was short in the early 40s until right after the war, when the bottom of my skirt was touching the top of my bobby socks. If you wore a sweater that was buttoned, you buttoned it down the back. And a string of pearls.*

*Eve: We lived on St. Charles Avenue for a while and I often took the streetcar to school. The streetcar was seven cents. My mother used to give me fifteen cents, and the cafeteria used to sell a caramel sucker for one cent, and that was my dessert every day.*

*Cathy: In the second half of my senior year, when we were all on the honor roll, at lunch we'd pile into whoever had the car and go to the snowball stand at Plum and Burdette. But we'd drive slowly down Freret because we all had beaus at Tulane and we'd "accidentally" bump into them.*

*Guess what happened at my graduation! One girl sat on her hoop and her skirt went straight up in the air over her head. She was trying her best to keep the thing down.*

*Eve: Miss Poole taught in Middle School. She was marvelous. She'd herd us on the streetcar to St. Roch cemetery by herself. Whatever she taught stayed with you.*

*Cathy: I never had a history teacher as inspiring as Wayne Frederick.*

*Eve: Mrs. Grout was the best, the strictest. She told me only Shakespeare could get an A from her.*

Listen to Katherine Talbot Holmquist '46 and Eugenia Seavey Shirley '46, best friends since childhood:

*Eugenia: I changed from McGehee's [an all-girls school] to Newman because my parents thought I should be exposed to boys.*

*Katherine: And man, was she exposed.*

*{The two women giggle with delight.}*

*Eugenia: We'd go sit on the back steps and watch the boys practice football.*

*Katherine: Boys were very important back then.*

*Eugenia: Patsy Brown Waters had the only car, and we loaded up and went downtown to a movie — skipping school — we thought we could do it and not get caught. Miss Christian was furious.*

*Katherine: Do you remember the movie we went to see? It was Hedy Lamar running naked through the woods with a gorilla chasing after her. But there were so many vines you couldn't see anything.*

*Eugenia: Every one of the operettas, we were always in. I was always in the chorus.*

*Katherine: I won the operetta award! For most improved.*

*Eugenia: We had lots of hayrides.*

*Katherine: During the year we'd have four to six.*

*Eugenia: We'd rent a banana wagon drawn by a horse. It would have sides but no tailgate.*

*Katherine: You'd go out to the lake on the hayrides. You had a date for this.*

*Eugenia: It was really fun — we'd sing songs, folk songs, school songs.*

*Katherine: I remember the drugstore around the corner from Newman. We'd go in the afternoons and try to read the magazines without paying.*

*Eugenia: They had these cute little ice cream tables. Now, the boys would go to a bar nearby, but we didn't go. We stood outside and sent messages in.*

*Katherine: We had a great childhood, I'll say that.*

*Eugenia: We enjoyed everything about the school — the academics as well as the play. Newman itself was so wonderful and friendly, it was like a big family.*

Social life at Newman centered on dances and hayrides, dates and parties, many hosted by organized groups such as sororities and fraternities. Much of it was good, clean fun. There were roller-skating parties that began at one person's house and wound up at Tulane, because the streets were smooth and free of potholes there. Afterward, everyone would return to the host's house for hot chocolate and cookies. Boys took girls on dates to the drugstore lunch counter, or to the movies at the Prytania Theater. Great quantities of hamburgers were consumed at Ye Olde College Inn and Camellia Grill. Groups got together for trips to Pontchartrain Beach or picnics on the levee. Carol Hart '43 remembers a party where the admission a boy paid was determined by the number of inches in his date's waist — a penny an inch. Of course, teenagers will be teenagers, even in that more innocent time. While some alumni don't recall anyone drinking alcohol, others say the boys drank, but the girls did not.

New Orleans was, of course, a segregated town in the thirties and forties — but it wasn't only blacks and whites who didn't interact. Much of Mardi Gras, and therefore, a large part of "society," was off limits to Jews, no matter how old or wealthy the family. This created a unique set of issues at Newman, surely the most religiously mixed school in the city.

"From the time you started at Newman until seventh grade, your friends were both," said Mrs. Kahn, meaning both Jewish and non-Jewish. "My very best friends were Christians." But by junior high, "Mardi Gras began to raise its ugly little head," Mrs. Hirsch said.

"At all of our out-of-school events from then on, we pretty much went out with the Jewish kids," Mrs. Kahn continued. "But in school, in classes, during the day, I was really still friendly with my Christian friends."

"They used to call that the five o'clock curtain," said Mrs. Hirsch. "But we knew who we were. We came from old, established New Orleans families too. We had our own lives. And our parents were socially active in the community."

It began in seventh or eighth grade, when gentile girls would join Eight O'Clocks, Nine O'Clocks and Subdebs, all clubs which hosted parties. Jewish boys often were invited to the parties, but Jewish girls were not. Fraternities and sororities, which were segregated by religion, flourished in high schools nationwide in that era, and they were a central part of life at Newman.

"That was fun," said Mrs. Shirley. "We had meetings every Saturday in people's homes, and after the meetings, we'd meet on the streetcar line to go downtown to movies — with our hair in curlers!"

Curlers were a badge of honor — it meant you had a date that night.

Carol Hart '43 grew up in the Home and loved his involvement with a Jewish fraternity. "I was fortunate to be in Tau Beta Phi, because there weren't many kids from the Home in any fraternities, especially that one," he said. "They must have waived my dues, because I had no money. Serving in the fraternity was an education in itself. Despite whatever the knocks are against fraternities, I was a freshman and I got to go to fraternity meetings on Sunday nights, and I was thrown in with older boys and I learned the art of debate and of expressing one's convictions."

His good memories extend to his whole experience at Newman; he never felt isolated or excluded for being a Home kid or for being Jewish. "There was no feeling, absolutely no feeling of differentiation," he said.

Tom Lewis '55, who is not Jewish, has a different view of fraternities. "They were horrible," he said. "There were Jewish fraternities and gentile fraternities and there was no crossover. They classified kids and grouped them into subgroups." If it hadn't been for these groups, he said, he would have been oblivious to the religious differences among his friends. "There would have been no distinction," he said.

Mr. Kohlmeyer has a softer view. "I think the school was remarkable for the mix that it had," he said. "It just worked. Back then, people socialized up to a point. In this town the doors always closed at night [to Jews]. There were fraternities, and they were always along religious lines. But it didn't seem to be a troublesome issue."

Jews and non-Jews agree that Newman did nothing to encourage the segregation that existed in New Orleans social circles. And while fraternities and sororities weren't banned until the late 1950s — when they were banned in most high schools — any other socializing that smacked of exclusion was investigated.

"We got in trouble once because they thought we were discriminating," said Katherine Talbot Holmquist.

*For our graduation, a bunch of us got together and decided we didn't want to go to the graduation party in the gym. So we had another party at the Audubon Tea Room. After graduation, Mr. Henson called me in and wanted to know if we were doing that to exclude the Jews. I told him that was not the case at all. It was because we could smoke and drink and we couldn't do that at the gym. He said, "Oh. Aren't you a little young for that?"*

During the war years, many extracurricular activities were scaled back or put on hold as everyone pitched in to aid the war effort. By 1942, the science club was collecting paper, seventh graders gathered tin foil, and eighth-grade boys, coat hangers. Junior girls knit sweaters and senior girls rolled bandages. One year, the juniors and seniors raised more than $21,000 buying defense bonds and stamps. In 1944, Newman's Red Cross pledged to make 200 Christmas stockings for soldiers, but wound up sending 376 because they collected so many goodies. That same year, eighth-grade girls collected 200 "phonograph" records for the soldiers. Kids saved the foil out of their parents' cigarette packages and made big balls out of it. People drove as little as possible; some Newman parents even moved closer to the school so their children could walk there, and it wasn't

*War bond sign, World War II, downtown New Orleans. (From the Historic New Orleans Collection, 1979.325.4087.)*
INSET: Pioneer *cover, May, 1944.*

unheard of to walk all the way to Pontchartrain Beach from Uptown. Eugenia Seavey Shirley "entertained" the troops. Her family invited service men home for Christmas one year, and she and Mrs. Holmquist did their best to attract their attention. Since they were still just girls, they now suspect they were simply annoying.

Ann Marie Gandolfo Smith '53 filled boxes that were sent to Europe, full of toothbrushes and other basics. "The vision of it going all the way across the ocean and imagining some deprived child getting it — I really wanted to make it special," she said.

Joe Epstein '48 said his class knit socks for soldiers one year: "I feel sorry for the poor bastard who got my socks."

Mrs. Kahn's family moved across the street from Newman during the war to save money on gas, and she said her mother ran a teen canteen and hosted dances, sock hops, anything to keep the girls from going downtown, "because there were sailors down there," she said. Doucette Cherbonnier Pascal, a biology teacher from 1939 to 1951, remembers students bringing her ducks and other game, "to get in good," because it was so hard to get meat during the war.

There were, of course, many alumni fighting in the war, and at least one teacher. Chick Henson, the beloved lower school gym teacher and coach, left school in the spring of 1942 to report for duty in Norfolk, Virginia. He'd signed up to be a physical education director for the Navy.

Newman graduate Forbes Bastion '38 was reportedly

*Clarence "Chick" Henson '29, Clarence C. Henson's son and a Newman gym teacher and coach from 1935–1971.*

shooting down Japanese planes, according to the *Pioneer*. He wrote a letter to a senior, which the *Pioneer* published:

> *Pardner, have a big time and enjoy everything you can because it looks as if this war is going to go on long enough to give you a chance to hunt targets that shoot back, and believe me, it's a funny feeling the first time it starts shooting back, and tracer bullets go zinging by your head, and you hear the bullets striking the armor plate right behind you like someone hitting a tin can with a hammer.*

Moise Goldstein Jr. '44 wrote an essay on the draft being extended to eighteen- and nineteen-year-olds: "Will the law break up most colleges, and, therefore, stunt the education of a whole generation? Yes, maybe it will. But, which is better, to have a college education and be one of Hitler's slaves, or to live in a world that is free, and let education come after the war?"

The *Pioneer*'s "For the girls" column ran a questionnaire on how dating was affected by the war. "Because the boys are putting most of their money into war stamps, how much do you think they should spend on a date?" the column asked.

Popular songs at Newman included "Praise the Lord and Pass the Ammunition" and "Der Fuhrer's Face." The favorite book — and movie — was *Gone with the Wind*. The favorite radio show was *The Hit Parade* with Frank "Swoonatra," the *Pioneer* reported.

Boys began taking "war math" and extra science courses that might be important if they wound up in uniform. Girls were taking nursing and first aid classes. Physical education took on a boot camp quality and included wrestling, rope climbing and posture training. "During the war, we did all kinds of strange things," Joe Epstein said. "There was an obstacle course in gym class, which I hated, because I was always too fat to go over the climbing wall."

In January, 1943, Major Samuel Zemurray Jr. '28 became the first Newman graduate to die in the war, according to an article in the *Pioneer*. He was a commanding officer of a U.S. Air Force squadron, and he died when his plane struck a mountainside in North Africa. Unfortunately, he would not be the last Newman alumnus to die in the war. But there were good stories as well: Lieutenant Harry Blumenthal '35, who was called "Brother" at Newman, rescued American soldiers from a Japanese-held island. He recounted the soldiers he found — starving and in rags, many of them ill with malaria. Lt. Blumenthal's destroyer and the others in the rescue fleet barely escaped under a shower of Japanese bombs.

When the war ended, Newman, along with the rest of the world, tried to get back to normal. Newman re-organized clubs that had disbanded and welcomed back Chick Henson when he drove up in his little red Lincoln Zephyr. Legendary history teacher Wayne Frederick, fresh from the war, arrived in the fall of 1946.

And it was time to get back to the serious business of pranks. Ed Roddy '49 remembered several infamous stunts that were pulled off in the late forties:

*They had these things they called window poles —*
*it had a little hook on the end of it and the window*
*latches had a circular grasp, so you'd reach up with the*
*pole to open them. A window was open one day so one of*
*the guys reached out the window with the pole and*
*caught one of the telephone wires. The objective was to*
*shoot it like an arrow onto the tennis courts. Instead, it*
*spun around all the wires and created a short circuit*
*and exploded the transformers all down the block. The*
*elementary school kids came screaming out of their*
*classes because of the explosions.*

And here's another one: A Newman neighbor kept chickens in his yard, so one day, some Newman students "borrowed" one. They took it to study hall and hid it in the drawer of the elderly, retired teacher in charge. Sometime during the class period, she opened the drawer and the chicken stuck its head out. She stomped out of the room to fetch the principal, but while she was gone, the kids threw the chicken out the window. When she returned, she opened the empty drawer with a righteous flourish. The children, when asked by the principal, had no knowledge of any chicken, naturally. The chicken's fate is, to this day, a mystery.

Not that pranks were limited to this era: C. Allen Favrot '43 and Harold B. Patterson '43 rigged the wiring of the bells so they could call a fire drill or dismiss class whenever they liked. They were written up in a fake newspaper, printed at a souvenir shop in the French Quarter, for being "arrested for wire fraud."

In the fifties, the pranks got even bolder: A group of kids once parked a fellow student's small car inside the school — on the second floor of the Jefferson Building. Things other than flags were always going up the flag pole: Garbage cans, a bicycle, and, in 1953, a student.

"Newman was great," Mr. Roddy said. "Pure fun."

*Woodcut calendar,*
*Arts Class 1946.*

HOMEWORK

INITIATION

JITTERBUG

TRYING ON CLOTHES

# A LITANY OF THE OLDEN DAYS

*BY BERTHE MARKS AMOSS '43*

*After graduating from Newman, Berthe Marks Amoss attended Newcomb College and Tulane, and holds a master's degree in English and art. She has been a teacher, an illustrator, a designer and an author of children's picture books and young adult novels. Her talents and accomplishments are many: she is the author of* The Cajun Gingerbread Boy *and* A Cajun Little Red Riding Hood, *to name just two of her numerous published works. From 1982 to 1994, she taught children's literature at Tulane and wrote a column, "Reading, Writing and Children," for* The New Orleans Times-Picayune. *She is a product developer for More Than a Card, Inc. and Cocodrie Press, LLC. She designs Advent calendars for the National Gallery of Art, the National Cathedral, The Metropolitan Museum of Art and others. She has taught and written books on how to write and illustrate children's literature. Most recently, she has expanded Tulane's children's literature program, Trial Balloons, and started a new line of children's books. Somehow, she also found time to raise six boys. She is married to James Amoss, and they live in New Orleans and in Pass Christian.*

I SKIPPED MIDDLE AGE. I had a lovely, leisurely childhood, a short miserable adolescence, and finally grew up close to my fortieth birthday. Now, suddenly, I am seventy-eight, an old lady.

Old age offers few consolations but one is the spectacular view over the twentieth century from on top a mountain of generations and lived history. I love remembering those remote years before WWII, depression years living in my grandparents' roomy house, grand central station for family, friends, relatives, neighborhood kids, and across the street from the boy I married fifty-seven years ago.

The New Orleans I knew was like a series of small towns. I lived in Uptown where families had known each other for generations. My childhood friends are still my friends, brought together by our parents' decision to send their children to Newman.

Just as 9/11 changed everything for the present generation, so December 7, 1941 changed it for us, sixteen at the time. My grandchildren call that pre-WWII time "The Olden Days."

Here then is my litany of the vanished Olden Days:

When you could go anywhere in New Orleans on the streetcar for seven cents and five cents bought a Coca-Cola, an ice cream cone, or a pack of Wrigley's chewing gum.

When my telephone number was Walnut 6388 and my young uncle, Bobby, and his friend, Julius, almost blew up the attic with a chemistry experiment.

When grass was something that grew in Greentrees, gay was a form of happiness, fun was a noun and cool described a few days in January.

When our whole family had just one doctor and he made house calls.

When the Jewish Orphans' Home, a dark red, brick building straight out of Dickens, contributed Rose, Sarah, and Marguerite to our class, and I swapped my peanut butter sandwich for matzo.

When my father, captain of the 1913 Tulane football team, took me to every game and hated LSU with a terrible passion.

When Margie West's mother gave me *The Scarlet Pimpernel* to read and I fell madly in love with Percy, that elusive pimpernel, an impossibly romantic hero.

When at St. Rita's Sunday Mass, Father Walsh turned red in the face and banged on the pulpit, railing against parents who sent their children to "Godless (non-Catholic) schools" and I knew he meant me and my parents.

When at ten years old, I coveted a $15 dress at Gus Mayer, and my grandmother rode the streetcar downtown, looked at it, crossed over to D. H. Holmes, bought a pattern, eyelet lace, ribbon, and material for $6, came home and made an exact copy to my ever-lasting joy.

When at fourteen, I was allowed to wear lipstick and my father said in disgust, "Now you look just like everybody else," thus making my day.

When *Little Orphan Annie* on the radio sent Jane Dicks her secret decoding badge in exchange for two Ovaltine tops, but my mother refused to buy Ovaltine because it was "too stimulating" and Jane said it would not be fair to Little Orphan Annie to reveal her secret message to me.

When Tom Favrot, a new boy at school, walked into the classroom, spotted a familiar face, and using my grandmother's nickname for me, said "Hi, Puss!" a name that to my chagrin stuck with my classmates.

When each spring meant Mr. Cooksey's school production of a Gilbert and Sullivan operetta and daily rehearsals in the courtyard made the scores familiar to the entire student body.

When cheating was such a disgrace and so shameful in the minds of students that only a very few students did.

When Mrs. Frankenbush read to her fourth grade, *Toinette's Philip* and *Juan and Juanita,* two wonderfully exciting stories, totally incorrect politically.

When Mrs. Van Kirk introduced the sixth grade to a new book, *Caddie Woodlawn,* and turned reluctant readers into life-long readers.

When Mrs. Grout insisted on proper grammar in the "themes" we had to write and "creative writing" were words of the future.

When we were young and immortal and knew that life would only get better.

I cannot keep the nostalgia for the Olden Days out of my litany, but I have written it as best I can without sentimentality or judgment, as close as possible to the way things were, and although I cherish that past, I take great delight in the present, in my family, in New Orleans, and in Newman, the school that framed my life.

*The cover of a 1950s folder for class photos.*

CHAPTER FIVE

# *Heroes: Teachers in Newman's first 50 years*

*"Phenomenal."*

*"Dedicated."*

*"Top notch."*

*"I never had a college teacher that was better."*

*"Very old school."*

*"Just the world's nicest guy."*

*"We were in love with him."*

*"She was wonderful."*

*"Of all the influences on my life, outside of my parents, I can say there's no question he was the greatest."*

*"He was so cool."*

NEWMAN
SCHOOL
GRADE 4
NOV 1952
NEW ORLEANS

NEWMAN
SCHOOL
GRADE 4
JAN 1953
NEW ORLEANS

*Class of 1961 in fourth grade.*

M ISS CHRISTIAN. MISS POOLE. Miss Mizzi. Mr. Allee. Mrs. Grout. Mr. Frederick. Mr. Aker.

Ask Newman alumni from the first fifty years to reminisce about the school, and they immediately start naming teachers and cataloguing their attributes. This comes before stories of big games or dances, before memories of best friends or first kisses.

When he received the 2002–2003 Distinguished Alumnus award, Isidore Cohn Jr. chose to open his remarks by reading what he'd written in the *Pioneer* in 1938. It was an ode to teachers:

> *Our teachers have tried to instill in us a sense of civic pride, an interest in national and international affairs, a desire to achieve — to reach the heights, a sense of personal honor and pride, a sense of toleration. To the teachers, then, and naturally through them to the school, we owe our deepest and most heartfelt gratitude, our most sincere thanks.*

In his remarks, he said, "The very fact that I can recall their names is a testimony to what they stood for."

In 2003, at the age of 102, Buddy Kearny '18 was the school's oldest living graduate, and he could still list almost every teacher he'd had at Newman.

"The principal was Mr. C.C. Henson," he said. "Miss Lee was in fifth grade, and Miss Cohen in sixth grade. She had two boys at school. Miss Marks, she was a hell raiser. She was very strict. She wasn't very gentle. There was a math teacher . . . gosh, I've forgotten his name. Mr. Allee was one of our favorite teachers. The athletic coach was Monk Simons — everybody liked Monk."

Among the first beloved staffers was Joe Carson, known to the students as "Uncle Joe." He taught math and oversaw athletics from 1909 to 1920. Mr. Carson was known for his school spirit — he would harangue students who didn't buy tickets to games. The *Pioneer* once said that his priorities were such that "if you made a good play on the gridiron you were safe for that month in geometry, and if you made a touchdown you would surely pass." When Mr. Carson left, to become principal of a high school in Lake Charles, the *Pioneer* mourned the loss, saying the school had lost "something vital, something we had always associated with the Newman Manual Training School." Gone was his "cheery voice, the hail-fellow-well-met voice of Uncle Joe."

Zelia Catlett Christian began at Newman in 1906 and remained until her death in 1944. Born and raised on a plantation near St. Francisville, she attended Newcomb College and taught for a short time in the Lafayette public schools. When she first came to Newman, she taught nature study and gardening in the elementary school, and was responsible for starting the student garden, a school tradition for many years. She later taught biology, and became vice-principal in 1919. Miss Christian rarely missed a football game or a school play or Mr. Cooksey's operetta. After she died, the Newman Loyalty Prize was renamed the Zelia C. Christian Award, and to this day, it is given to students who attend every year at Newman.

An era of teaching legends began in the late 1920s. "They were top-notch, and they were the great influences on our lives," said Andrée Keil Moss '55. And, she said, echoing what many alumni say: "I didn't have to do any studying at all the first two years of college."

Some were "old school" — motherly women straight out of Central Casting who did little coddling, yet loved their students dearly. "They were career teachers," said David Stone '57. "They were no-nonsense, sensible women in sensible shoes with grey hair in buns who didn't take anything from anybody. They were terrific."

There was Eugenia Poole, a Middle School teacher at Newman from 1922 to 1953. A native of New Orleans, Miss Poole "looked like a bulldog," according to several alumni, but she was a warm and sensitive teacher. "She was wonderful," said William Rosen '54. When another teacher flunked him and threatened to hold him back a year, Mr. Rosen recalled, Miss Poole said, "Don't listen to that old woman."

Parents paid Miss Poole to take their children on vacations — a summer cruise, or a train ride to California. During the school year, she would take large groups of children on week-long trips around the state. Newman came to be known around Louisiana because of these journeys, called "Miss Poole's pilgrimages." They'd pile onto a Greyhound bus and see the Cajun prairies or swamps or plantations, sometimes going as far as Texas, with Miss Poole as the only chaperone. On one such excursion, a planter in Lafayette proposed to Miss Poole. "This man, admiring how effectively she handled her 40 students, wanted her as mother for his five," the *Pioneer* reported. "After hearing the man's tale of how his wife had died, leaving him with five youngsters, she calmly but tactfully said no."

Dr. Cohn was very ill as a child, confined to an oxygen tent and then at home for at least a month. He said Miss Poole came to see him every day, when he was well enough, and tutored him so he wouldn't fall behind.

"She had a very round face and eyes that looked right through you," said Sidney Pulitzer '53. "One time, she called me out after class, and she said, 'You're a very smart guy. You can accomplish anything.' Anyone who looked like that and told you that, you believed her. That changed my life."

A 1950 *Pioneer* feature on Miss Poole ended with this paragraph:

> *She says that if her pupils, as citizens of this city, could put New Orleans where it rightfully belongs, she would feel as though she had helped to do it and would be amply rewarded. Miss Poole adds that she loves children; but, when she gets to Heaven, if there is ONE angel under twenty, she'll "go the other way!"*

Pauline Mizzi taught sixth grade from 1922 to 1953. A native of Opelousas, she chain smoked and recited poetry to anyone who would listen. Her classroom often had a thick haze of smoke hanging in the air. She wore unique hats and told Cajun stories, and was fiercely dedicated to her students. She organized Little Women, a group for sixth grade girls that met every other Saturday in the members' homes. They discussed literature, committed poems to memory and studied the life of literary greats such as Henry Wadsworth Longfellow.

"Our loved and able teacher, Miss Mizzi, has taught us how to conduct our own meetings," reported the *Pioneer* in 1923. "And, most wonderful of all, she has shown us it is possible to gain knowledge and enjoy ourselves while doing it."

The girls did community service as well: In 1927, they sent care packages to the children affected by the Mississippi flood.

The Motto of the club was "To be the big women of tomorrow, we must be the real 'Little Women' of today."

In 1926, Miss Mizzi organized a new club: Manual's Good Fellows, for fifth and sixth grade boys. It was similar to the girls club, with some new additions. The boys learned public speaking, and each month they performed one "outstanding act of helpfulness" for an outsider.

Miss Mizzi also created the Mother's Day program, in which children would recite lines of Shakespeare or a famous speech and pin carnations on their mothers.

She wasn't an easy teacher, however.

"She was very autocratic," said Diana Monroe Lewis '55. She invited pranks as a result, Mrs. Lewis said. "One time we took a field trip to the Latter Library on St. Charles and when we got back, we sent a delegation up ahead of her to the classroom on the third floor of the Danneel Building. They set the clock forward so she'd think the bell had already rung. She let us out early."

Walter Goldsberry Allee taught science from the 1910s into the 1940s, and helped many of his students win national honors in an annual chemistry essay writing contest. He was always at school until at least 5 P.M., and he kept his laboratory open on Saturdays for students needing extra help. He helped set up Newman's first cafeteria, and was a fixture at football games. A pleasant, smiling man, he amused his students by addressing them in class as "Ladies, gentlemen and otherwise . . ." Some felt close enough to him to call him "Pops."

"He was my mentor — he was a Yankee by birth, but just as fine a person as you wanted to know," said Karlem Reiss '29, who taught physics at Tulane for more than fifty years.

Henriette Vallon Monrose '43 loved him even though she says she "blew up" his chemistry lab. "Mr. Allee said, 'I'll pass

CLOCKWISE FROM TOP LEFT: *Joe "Uncle Joe" Carson, a teacher from 1909 to 1920. Zelia Catlett Christian, teacher, administrator, 1906-1944. Eugenia Poole, Middle School teacher, 1922–1953. Walter Goldsberry Allee, science teacher from the 1910s to the 1940s. Mercedes Discon, a math teacher. Wayne and Edwina Frederick. Mr. Frederick was a history teacher from the late 1940s until 1962. Mrs. Frederick was the French teacher. Margaret Turner Grout, English teacher and department chair, 1928–1969.*

SIXTH GRADE - NEWMAN SCHOOL - 1949

TOP ROW: WOLCHANSKYS LAWSON; HAMER; PARKER; JORDEN; COHEN; GLAVERY; MOORE; MITCHEL; WAGNER; LASHLEY; RODDY

MID ROW + SPRINGER; PULITZER; WEGMAN; STARK; GRAFTON; LEJEUNE; SHEFFIELD; LEVY; KAHN; NEWMAND; KEIL
LEGENDGE; CAIRNS; CAHN; HERRON                                      HARMS; KARNO

MID ROW VILLIAMS; MONROE; LYLE; SLATTEN; REDDOCK; BAUMBACK; HERN; KESSLER; ZEMURRY; BORAH; GORDDEN +

LOW ROW WHITNEY; CLINGMAN; LEVY; WINN; ERMAN; DAVIS; WITTENBERG; WEINER; MAYS; HAYNES; ROSENBLUM; RITTENBERG

*Class of 1955 in Sixth grade.*

you and you just pass right out the door,'" she recalled.

Margaret Frankenbush and Olivia Ewing were the fourth grade teachers for many years. "Mrs. Ewing was an absolutely wonderful woman," Mr. Stone said. "She was handsome, with snow-white hair in braids pulled back on top of her head. She was very into ancient history, not just Greek and Roman but the other ancient civilizations. I have a distinct recollection of her going through two straight class periods on Hannibal's invasion of Italy and mapping it out on the blackboard."

Mrs. Frankenbush, known as "Frankie" to some, was another old-fashioned teacher, her students recalled. "She was a little bitty tiny thing and she wore pinch-nosed glasses," said Katherine Talbot Holmquist '46 of her fourth grade teacher. "She was very cute and sweet."

"She was tremendously respected," said Mr. Stone. "She somehow was able to command perfect discipline without ever raising her voice or saying anything particularly animated."

Carol Graves McCall '58 said Mrs. Frankenbush taught her fractions with a technique that stuck. "The way she taught us was to bring a pie to school," she said. "Well, you quickly learned that a sixteenth was smaller than an eighth."

No teacher from Newman's first half-century inspires more conversation than Margaret Turner Grout. "She was the school's infamous taskmaster," Dr. Marmelzat said. "It was known that the chance of receiving an 'A' from Miss Turner was as likely as hearing a sour note flying out of Louis Armstrong's trumpet. I desperately wanted her approval because I knew there would be great meaning behind it."

Born in Chicago, Margaret Turner was one of five children and went to a large, public school. Later, she majored in English and minored in Latin at the University of Chicago. She heard of Newman through a friend who taught there, and, taking a fill-in post that was supposed to last a year, she wound up staying three decades, except for a few years when she moved with her husband to Mississippi. In a 1939 *Pioneer* interview, she claimed she had no ambition as a child "except perhaps to become twenty-one years old." She said she decided in her junior year of college to become a teacher because she thought it would be "easy," but she soon discovered it was not. She said her favorite sport was football, and her favorite hobby was reading. She called grading papers her favorite recreation, and her favorite food was artichokes.

By 1962, Mrs. Grout was an educational leader in the city because of her emphasis on teaching composition and her early adoption of Advanced Placement English classes at Newman.

She was a notoriously tough grader. She would assign essays weekly and somehow managed to grade each one with remarkable care and attention. Alumni remember her returning papers that were drowning in a sea of red ink marks. Eve Godchaux Hirsch '44 said if a student made more than two spelling errors on a paper for Mrs. Grout, she would flunk that paper. "I never had a college teacher that was better than Mrs. Grout," she said. Many alumni agree. "Everybody was scared to death of her," said Eugenia Seavey Shirley '46. "I was so afraid, I didn't know if I liked her or not. I had a 'cute' habit of putting a little 'O' over my 'I,' and she screamed at me!"

One winter in the 1950s, it was snowing outside — a rare event in New Orleans — and Mrs. Grout, put out by her students' eyes wandering to the windows, rapped her pen on the blackboard and said, "You WILL pay attention! Keep your eyes forward!"

"Then Mr. Kalin came in and dismissed school for the rest of the day," Mrs. McCall said.

*"Little Women," Pauline Mizzi's club for Newman girls.*

Arthur Luerhmann '48 said Mrs. Grout wasn't what he'd call "a buddy:"

> *I can't say I was in love with her, but she wasn't a disciplinarian, she was a strict practitioner. I earn a living now writing computer books, and I didn't even think I could write. But Mrs. Grout was a pusher. I thought of myself as a failure as a writer until I got to college and realized I was way up there. And that was her training in the basics of writing.*

After World War II, a new teaching style emerged — more modern, provocative and intimate. These were teachers who inspired a kind of idol worship, but who also might invite students to their homes after school. Wayne Frederick, a history teacher, arrived in the late 1940s and became the center of a group of the most intellectual Newman students. Carmel Cohen '50 described a final exam he gave:

> *For our final examination in a history course, we walked in and on the board all it said was, "Sarajevo: Before and After. Please Comment." We could take as many blue books as we wanted, we could go anywhere we wanted, and we could hand it in by midnight at his house.*

Mr. Frederick was born in South America and moved to the United States when he was ten years old. He lived in Missouri and eventually attended Missouri State Teacher's College and later the University of Wisconsin. He enlisted during World War II, and was assigned to teach in Puerto Rico; shipping out of New Orleans, he got a taste of the city and decided it was where he wanted to live after the war.

Mr. Frederick liked to shatter the godlike images of the founding fathers by telling controversial stories about them. He'd talk about the "filthy bourgeoisie" and criticized President Franklin D. Roosevelt.

"He hated Roosevelt," said Doug Forsyth '53. "He referred to him as 'the great wind that blew through the White House.' "

"I remember him talking about [the French Empress] Josephine and he would imitate how she talked, because she had bad teeth," said Patricia Kennedy Livingston '53.

"Wayne Frederick and John Aker, who taught English, were the kinds of teachers who made changes in your life," said Tom Lewis '55. "I was kind of coasting through and Wayne Frederick took me aside and said I was the laziest student he'd ever had and he'd been teaching for years, and if I didn't straighten up, he was going to cane me, basically. He was extremely disciplined and he disciplined the students."

Mr. Frederick did not take a universal interest in students, however. "I was not one of his brilliant students — it was almost as if he didn't notice me," said Mrs. McCall. But he had a significant impact on those students he did notice. "Of all the influences on my life, outside of my parents, I can say there's no question he was the greatest influence," said David Stone. "His teaching style was so sophisticated and engaging, and he was so perceptive and so interested in us."

Mr. Frederick, who was married to Newman's French teacher, would have students to his house for intellectual discussions. As coach of the debate team, he accompanied students around the state for competitions. "We traveled to small towns and sat around until two in the morning at some little hotel and talked about Eastern mysticism, or whatever he wanted to talk about," Mr. Stone said. "We'd smoke cigars and talk about things like whether, with enough strength of belief, you could walk through a wall."

Mr. Frederick left in 1962 to teach at Phillips Academy (Andover), a New England boarding school, where he also enjoyed a cult following among his students. He would return to Newman in the 1980s, but didn't stay long before retiring.

Some students loved the French teacher, Edwina Frederick, more than her husband. "I learned more French than I could possibly imagine," said Louis Fishman '59. "When we began in seventh grade, after the first six weeks of class, you could speak no English. If you did, you had to put a penny or something like that in a jar, and at the end of the year we used it to go on a picnic. But we were fluent."

John Aker, an English teacher who began at Newman in 1948 at the age of twenty-five, was worshipped by some as intensely as Mr. Frederick. He was a fierce intellectual who was considered so cool he could hurl disdainful remarks — and even inanimate objects — at his students with impunity. He spent his summers at Bread Loaf College at the feet of poet Robert Frost, who would read his new poems aloud, provided no one took notes. Mr. Aker would sit out of sight and take notes anyway.

"To this day I can recall, he just took us through *Tom Sawyer, Huckleberry Finn, Moby Dick*, and he taught us how to enjoy books — we were in love with him," said Andrée Moss.

He made *Julius Caesar* come alive for William Rosen. "He read it to us," he said. "I can still see him talking about the Roman crowd listening to Octavius — the Roman crowd eating raw onions for breakfast. He made it alive."

"He was so cool," said Ann Marie Gandolfo Smith '53. "He would actually dance with the girls at dances. He would smoke in his car during lunch. We sat outside on the neutral ground during lunch, and we'd go talk to him and see him smoking and it was like ooh! So exciting."

Tom Lewis remembers a terrifying Mr. Aker: "In the beginning of class, he gave you a list of words, and usage and punctuation rules, and in addition, he said spelling had to be perfect. From then on, if you gave him an essay that wasn't technically perfect, he'd kill you. He'd take off 15 points for a missing comma."

Mr. Lewis remembers reading "The Bear" by William Faulkner and Ernest Hemingway's *The Old Man and the Sea,* which was serialized in Life magazine at the time. Normally, Mr. Aker's senior class would read *Moby Dick,* Mr. Lewis said. "But he regarded our class as so stupid that he waived the requirement." Mr. Stone remembers Mr. Aker as a "gruff, outspoken guy who hated giving us writing assignments. He said, 'I don't do that because I can't stand reading what you write.'"

He had a few memorable quirks. "His biggest pet peeve in the world was being told he looked like Orson Wells, but he did," said Patricia Livingston. Mr. Aker kept a frog on his desk — made of pottery or jade, no one can recall — that he would use as a sort of attention-getter. "If he didn't like your answer, he'd throw it at you," said Doug Forsyth. "And you held that frog until you redeemed yourself. Once, a girl ducked and it went out the window — he never forgave her."

Many years later, after Mr. Aker left Newman for a school in Texas, Jane Bruce Jenevein '53 got a chance to tell her beloved English teacher how much he meant to her. They happened to be in the same hospital one night in 1969, both awaiting surgery the next morning. When Mrs. Jenevein discovered he was there, she put on her robe, padded down the hall, and found him.

"I said, 'Mr. Aker, you were the best teacher I ever had,' Mrs. Jenevein recalled, her eyes filling with tears. "I cried, and he cried too." He died about six months later.

*Eddy Kalin, math teacher and principal, and Angela Devlin, art teacher and Lower School head, with a group of students.*

hidden scandal: Mr. Kalin was often teased in the *Pioneer* for his admiration of the opposite sex. In a 1946 interview with the *Pioneer*, he was asked why girls shouldn't be allowed to wear slacks to school. His answer: "Too concealing."

In the 1950s, space exploration was still years away, but one Mercedes Discon, a math teacher, was obsessed. "From the moment we walked into class, she talked about men going to the moon," said William Rosen. "We all thought she was crazy."

"She had a space ship hanging from the ceiling in her classroom," said Louis Fishman. "And she believed that parallel lines would meet on the moon. Someone then tied little plastic cowboy and Indian figures to the ship. So while you sat in class, you had this notion of a ship going to the moon, with cowboys and Indians on it who would observe the meeting of parallel lines."

Some teachers are remembered for their not-so-secret "human" sides. One teacher smoked in a storeroom off his laboratory, thinking no one could smell it wafting into the adjoining classrooms. Another kept a flask in her cabinet. Eddy Kalin, a revered math teacher and later the principal, was thought to have a soft spot for pretty girls, who would sit up front in the hopes of getting good grades. This was no great

Doucette Cherbonnier Pascal, who taught biology from 1939 to 1951, said the size of the school encouraged the teachers to be very involved in their students' lives. "We all had a personal interest in the students," she said. "All the teachers stayed after school, every day."

Dr. Cohn summed up the feelings of so many alumni when he said: "I think all of us would like to be remembered as favorably as they are."

*RIGHT: Class of 1953 tours Louisiana and Texas in 1949.*

*Class of 1964, in fourth grade, staging a puppet show.*

# CHAPTER SIX

# A Milestone —
# Newman at Fifty

Beginning with kindergarten, each student is treated
as an individual to whom education must be fitted;
Newman does not believe its students must conform to
a predetermined pattern.

EXCERPT FROM A BOOKLET
CELEBRATING NEWMAN'S FIFTIETH ANNIVERSARY

A FTER THE WAR, NEW ORLEANS changed — albeit slowly — and Newman changed. Veterans came home, bringing with them housing and job shortages and a baby boom. Mayor deLesseps S. "Chep" Morrison got New Orleans back in working order, creating jobs and fixing streets and buildings that had been neglected during the war. In 1948, WDSU-TV broadcast the city's first television program.

In 1946, the Home stopped housing children and began its transition into the Jewish Children's Regional Service. In the process, the Home essentially gave Newman to Newman: the school became independent, incorporated as a non-profit entity. The new charter called for Newman to remain coeducational and open to all students without regard to creed. The school considered buying the building that housed the Home, as a place to expand the campus, but in the end it was sold to the Jewish Community Center. The JCC tore down the Home and rebuilt a new facility in the 1960s. The JCRS stayed there rent-free until 1988; the organization then paid rent for twelve years before moving in 2000 to Causeway Boulevard.

At about the same time, after thirty-five years at the school, Mr. Henson announced his retirement as of January 1947. It took many events to say goodbye properly. On January 8,

*LEFT: Newman's Cafeteria, 1948.*

*Clarence Henson's retirement, 1946. Copyright 2003 The Times-Picayune Publishing Co., all rights reserved. Used with permission of the* Times-Picayune.

1947, in honor of his seventy-second birthday, Newman held a special birthday assembly for Mr. Henson. The president of the Student Council gave him a silver tray engraved "Presented to Mr. C.C. Henson by the Newman student body in loving appreciation of his unselfish work for the school." Later that day, the elementary school gave him a leather desk set. That night, the faculty held a banquet in the library, decorated with greens and camellias, and presented him and his wife with a silver tea service. On February 6, the Parent-Teacher Association and the board of trustees hosted a reception for Mr. and Mrs. Henson in the home of Mr. and Mrs. Fernand C. Gandolfo. They gave him a check for $1,397 and a poem by Angela Devlin, engraved and written on scroll. The board named him Director Emeritus. The debate club was reorganized and named the Henson Oratorical Society, led by Mr. Frederick.

"The steady rise of Newman has been largely a reflection of his talents and industry," said the editors of *The States-Item* when Mr. Henson retired. "Discriminating observers in schools and colleges rate him one of Louisiana's most outstanding educators."

When Mr. Kalin succeeded Mr. Henson, tuition was $175 for a kindergartener and $350 for a senior. There were about 680 students enrolled. Eddy Stephen Kalin, a pleasant, intellectual man with a silly sense of humor and a wide range of talents, was born in Sweden in 1900, but came to the United States as a child. He went to high school in Connecticut, where he was a member of the state championship football and debate teams. He signed up for the Army in 1918 and was stationed in Vermont with the Students Army Training Corps. He attended Middlebury College in Vermont, graduating magna cum laude in 1923 with majors in English and math and minors in physics and chemistry. He played varsity football, was president of the

*Eddy S. Kalin, Newman's principal, 1947–1964.*

student body, was elected Phi Beta Kappa and was nominated for a Rhodes scholarship. After graduation, he became the assistant dean of English at Bread Loaf summer school, which was affiliated with Middlebury, while earning his master's degree in math. He then took a teaching job at a private school in

*Original Stern Building completed in 1948, a gift of Percival Stern (inset).*

Pennsylvania — but just for a year. In 1925, he came to Newman as the math teacher. Somehow, he also found time to earn another master's degree from Teacher's College at Columbia and to do graduate work at Harvard University.

At Middlebury, he met his wife, Beryle Gaylor, to whom he wrote love poems on her birthday and on anniversaries. Mrs. Kalin became a well-known figure in New Orleans; she was active in several charitable organizations and sang for more than fifty years — well into her eighties, despite being almost completely deaf her whole life — with the New Orleans Opera Association. They had two daughters who attended Newman: Beryle '49 and Karen '51.

At Newman, Mr. Kalin, an admired and accomplished math teacher, quickly became head of the math department and

remained in that position until he became principal in 1947. That year, Newman was showing signs of age and space was getting tight. Thanks to a $150,000 gift from Percival Stern, a new Lower School building was in the works; it promised to be the most modern school building in the city, with special child-sized furnishings, radiant heating and glass panels that opened up to give the inside an outdoor feel. "I remember when the Stern Building was brand-new," said Angus Lind '62. "I remember walking in and thinking it was so cool."

But the school needed much more, including a new heating system, new plumbing, toilets, an auditorium, more classrooms, roofing and electrical work. So in 1948, the first fund drive in the school's history was announced. People had given money through the years, of course; the library, for example, was named for Rebecca Grant Popp after she gave the school a large bequest in 1928. But this was the first time Newman had formally passed the hat. The school asked parents, alumni and friends for $350,000, publicizing the need in a pamphlet and in the newspapers. "Why Funds for Newman School Must Be Raised Now!" the pamphlet said. "Today Newman School is Facing a Crisis!"

At the time, the school's annual budget was $188,500, roughly equal to what was coming in, between tuition and investments. There was no money for extras such as repairs and new buildings.

The fund drive raised $125,000, enough for the campus to see many improvements, including new science labs and a motion picture projection room, and renovations to the Jefferson, Valmont and Saratoga buildings. The PTA raised money for the Zelia C. Christian Faculty Room.

In the late forties, Newman students spent a lot of ink in the *Pioneer* discussing whether to introduce a formalized honor system. In 1950, the Student Council announced a two-part code of honor. The first part was a voluntary oath taken by the students:

> I hereby promise never to bring disgrace to Newman School by failure to enforce the standards of Honor Super Omnia. The ideals of Newman will I ever uphold, and defend, at any time and in any place.
>
> The spirit and principles of this school, which have been maintained over the years, will I strive to enhance and further to the best of my ability.

The second part of the code stated that students were expected to report the "dishonorable acts" of their fellow students. The council set up a box in which students could record violations on small white cards bearing the inscription, "Newman Honor." Or, violations could be reported to the Student Council or a teacher. Violations included copying, talking during a test, plagiarizing, stealing, vandalism, and warning later classes of pop quizzes. "It was a very serious undertaking," said Carmel Cohen '50. "It was based on detailed and scholarly research."

On a lighter note, in 1948, Newman captured four Riverside crowns — in football, basketball, track and tennis — an unprecedented feat. And in May 1950, an anonymous donor gave Newman $100,000 to build a new boys' gym. The announcement came during the annual Dads Club athletic banquet at Lenfant's Boulevard Room. The gym, to be designed by Solis Seiferth and Julius Dreyfous, would be at Danneel and Valmont streets. The Dads Club raised money for the old gym to be refurbished for the girls and for use as a soundproof band room. Around the same time, Newman bought property on Danneel and Valmont streets and closed Valmont to traffic, as it is today. The new boys' gym opened in 1951.

The year 1950 also saw the first Alumni Day and the first class trip to Washington, D.C. Miss Poole took twenty-two students to the nation's capital. A Lower School student government called "Pow-Wow" formed, with members elected four times a year, to ensure lots of children had a chance to practice leadership.

In 1953, as Newman approached its fiftieth birthday, tuition ranged from $250 to $460, and almost all graduates went to college. Newman's stated philosophy emphasized a tailor-made education for each child. "Beginning with kindergarten, each student is treated as an individual to whom education must be fitted," stated the booklet published in honor of

*First staff of the Greenie, the student newspaper, 1955.*

*Girls Good Government, known as Tri-G, 1954.*

the fiftieth anniversary. "Newman does not believe its students must conform to a predetermined pattern."

President Dwight Eisenhower was in the White House, Robert F. Kennon was Louisiana's governor, and Chep Morrison was in the middle of his fifteen-year run as mayor of New Orleans. The city was growing by leaps and bounds, expanding outward into newly forming suburban neighborhoods. American soldiers were coming home from the Korean Conflict, Jonas Salk had invented the polio vaccine, and segregation had been ruled illegal. A report said cigarettes cause cancer; kids at Newman, however, were smoking more than ever before. It was fashionable for girls to bleach their hair and wear heavy "pancake" makeup, and the class of 1954 dedicated the "senior number" *Pioneer* to Isidore Newman, in honor of the fiftieth anniversary.

Some of the charming, old-fashioned things about New Orleans, and Newman, began to disappear. The city grew larger and more suburban. By 1955, construction had begun on bridges across Lake Pontchartrain and the Mississippi River. Neighborhood groceries began to close as supermarkets opened, and the street vendors became rarer. A new city hall and a new airport were built. During Newman's renovations, acoustic-tile ceilings and fluorescents lights changed the look inside the old buildings, and modern green boards replaced blackboards. The Jefferson Building went from having two entrances to just one, as it is today. No one ate lunch on the neutral ground anymore. Many of the elderly women who had taught at Newman for generations retired.

And one of Newman's oldest "students" passed away. For more than a decade, a dog named Butch, an Airedale-Irish Terrier mix, had been coming to school, attending classes and befriending anyone generous with caresses or lunch. At first,

he accompanied his master, Joe Friend '49, beginning around 1943. He behaved like a dog initially, waiting for Mr. Friend outside, standing watch over the boy's bicycle. But that became tiresome, so he began going inside, wandering into classrooms in search of Mr. Friend. He developed a routine — toast with Mr. Soyka, lunch with students, and so on. Mr. Henson wasn't crazy about the dog, and tried to "expel" him several times, to no avail. But Mr. Kalin and Butch had a friendly understanding.

"He was amused by him," said Mr. Friend. Butch continued to "attend" Newman long after Mr. Friend graduated. An issue of the *Pioneer* was dedicated to him, and when he died in 1954, the *Pioneer* wrote:

> One Saturday morning shortly before he died, he made a last trip to Newman to see his friend Mrs. Nick. The effort for him was a great one, and he was carried home panting. Soon afterwards, Butch died quietly of what seemed to have been a heart condition. He will be greatly missed by his friends at Newman.

He was also written up in the debut issue of the *Greenie*, a new weekly student newspaper. The headline on the first issue of the *Greenie*, published on September 24, 1954, proudly announced, "Birth of a Newspaper."

"Hold on to your copy!" a lead article said. "It may be worth a fortune some day as a rare first edition."

The *Greenie* promised not to detract from the monthly *Pioneer* but rather enhance its popularity, "by eliminating stale news." It had a gossip column with items such as who was "swinging at the Phi Delta Theta rush party." There was sports news, detailing plays on the gridiron by Jerry "The Ugly Dragon" Favrot and Dink "The Duke of Gretna" Samuels.

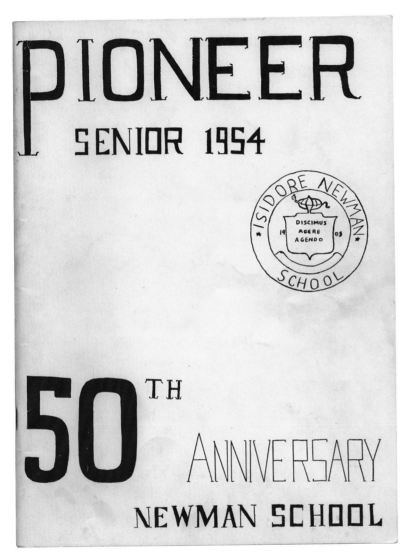

*1954* Pioneer, *dedicated to Isidore Newman in honor of the school's fiftieth anniversary.*

# The Greenie

*Published by the Newman Council*

| Volume 1 | September 24, 1954 | Number 1 |

## BIRTH OF A NEWSPAPER

Here's the first issue of the first printed weekly newspaper ever published by Newman students. Hold on to your copy! It may be worth a fortune some day as a rare first edition.

This new publication will give up-to-date news each week about all sports, social events, and other school functions. It will also be a needed means for presenting current problems which may arise to students, faculty, and administration in a comprehensive and interesting way. Are you interested in knowing who was somewhere and with whom last weekend? Or do you want to know what the Newman Council is doing? You will find all this in your newspaper.

Some of you are probably thinking that such a paper will detract from the *Pioneer*. This is not true. In fact, it should help make the monthly magazine more enjoyable to both its readers and writers by eliminating stale news.

By this time, you should be able to see why this paper must be a success. This success will depend largely upon hard work on the part of the staff. Mostly, however, this success depends upon you; yes, upon you and your support. If you have any constructive suggestions, please make them either to a member of the Newman Council or to a member of the staff. It was through much time, work, and effort on the part of the Executive Board and Mr. Thomas this summer that this paper came into being. But remember, this is

your paper. Its success is up to you. The staff is willing to work, if you will back them up with your wholehearted support and enthusiasm.

### IN MEMORIAM

We sadly announce the death of "Butch" during the summer vacation. After more than fourteen years of regular attendance at Newman, this loyal mascot passed to his canine reward. He will be grieved for by students, alumni, and faculty.

### SLAY SLIDELL

By special arrangement there will be no mosquitoes at the game tonight and, since NORD is on this side of the river, let's all be there to back up the Greenie big team against our perennial rival, Slidell. WHIP THEM TIGERS, BOYS, WHIP 'EM!

*The first* Greenie, *1954.*

Tom Lewis '55 was a founding editor of the *Greenie*. He started it by himself one semester, but was soon joined by Sidney Shushan '55 as co-editor. It was printed in green ink, which Mr. Lewis said he thought was very clever at the time.

There also was an underground senior paper called *The Stoolie*, said Louis Fishman '59. Modeled after the *Tattler* of the Revolutionary War, it was a primitive, mimeographed publication, mostly full of gossip.

Mr. Fishman remembers a magical moment in the fifties when the cafeteria went from being a dingy place with the same menu every week — red beans and rice on Mondays, meatballs and spaghetti on Wednesdays, etc. — to being a bright, modern facility run by Morrison's, the cafeteria chain. "It turned into a fancy line," Mr. Fishman said. "The first thing you saw was multi-colored drinks — they were pink and they were purple and they were lemon colored. And dessert was the second thing you came across in the line. That was fun."

Social lives were modernizing as well. Andrée Keil Moss '55 and Diana Monroe Lewis '55 remember hosting parties for their entire class in their homes. Everyone would play ping-pong in the basement and go swimming, and often, the parents were conspicuously absent. Graduation was an all-night affair, at the end of which kids often would return to Newman and pull a prank.

David Stone '57 recalls "a great deal of drinking" at dances and parties. It wasn't taboo, he said. At a Garden District home after a party in junior high, he remembers the mother offering around a tray of Crème de Menthe frappes for the kids. "The notion of drinking as a social evil wasn't really prevalent," he said. "I went to a lot of social teas, but I never saw anybody drink tea. Not a cup of tea was in sight."

Tom Lewis said he and his friends began drinking around ninth grade. "It was like a switch turned on in ninth grade and you started drinking," he said. "You could go to any bar, and if you had a quarter you could buy a drink. "

Fraternities and sororities continued to flourish and stir up controversy until May 23, 1957, when school officials sent a letter to "patrons and students of Newman school" announcing that the board had met the day before and adopted a resolution to ban sororities and fraternities. They had already been banned earlier that year at McGehee's, Country Day and Sacred Heart. St. Martin's officials were discussing a similar ban.

A group of Newman parents protested, saying the ban was "ill-advised" and amounted to "an intrusion upon the authority of parents to regulate the off-campus social activities of their children."

"When they did away with fraternities, everyone was so appalled," said Carol Graves McCall '58. "But in retrospect, they were hurtful to children and the activities often ended up with a lot of drinking."

Racial segregation persisted in New Orleans, as it did throughout the South in the fifties, despite new laws. Mr. Lewis said he rarely saw a black person. "I traveled all over the state for four years in high school to play all these games and I never saw a black face. Never. And it was never even talked about."

Another rarely-crossed line was the one between the "frats" and the "cats," Mr. Lewis said. The frats wore white bucks and white socks, khaki pants and white shirts with the sleeves rolled up. They lived Uptown or in the Garden District and usually went to private or parochial schools. The cats wore suede shoes and slicked back their hair; they lived in the Irish Channel and went to public school.

"You could always tell a frat from a cat, and you didn't want to be caught alone in cat country by the cats," he said.

*Henson Oratorical Society in the 1950s.*

*Class of 1950.*

*A reenactment of the Louisiana Purchase, Class of 1957.*

109

# LUCKY ME

BY CAMILLA TRINCHIERI '60

*Born in Prague to an American mother and an Italian diplomat father, Camilla came to New Orleans as a teenager, graduated from Newman and then Barnard College before returning to Italy. In Rome she worked in the movie industry as a dubbing producer\ director with directors such as Federico Fellini, Luchino Visconti and Lina Wertmüller.*

*Camilla came back to New York City in 1980, married, received a Masters of Fine Arts degree from Columbia University and became an American citizen. She has published seven mysteries as well as several short stories under her own name and the pseudonym Camilla T. Crespi. She had her first art show in September in a Manhattan cafe and will have a solo show in November 2004 at St. Francis College in Brooklyn Heights.*

SEPTEMBER, 1954 — the school year had started when my father, two sisters and I arrived in New Orleans. Italian and Catholic, my father thought his youngest daughter needed the strictures of the Sacred Heart School. That's where luck comes in. Seventh grade at that venerable institution on St. Charles Avenue was full. What to do, my father asks his new acquaintances? Luck plays her hand again. "Do you want to send her to the very best school in this city?" a blessed person asks. "Isidore

Newman!" My father followed that advice, and never regretted it. Neither did I.

At first, I was a little scared. A new country to fit into, new friends to be made, a new curriculum I might drown in. My English had holes in it. Poised Mrs. Schultz, our Upper School principal, with tiny feet I marveled at, took me under her wing. Life at Newman was all about possibilities offered, she said. The teachers would cheer me on, but the rest was up to me. Periodically, throughout my five Newman years, she would ask how I was doing. I never sought her advice (what teenager does?), but I knew her office was always open — a reassurance I badly needed.

I plunged into the possibilities, eager to make them realities. I learned to jitterbug at my first dance with a blond boy, the Donald O'Connor of the class, whose name I don't remember. I ran for class office with Richard Stone's encouragement, sang pitifully in the Gilbert and Sullivan operettas where Richard's brother, David, reigned supreme. I raced around the baseball field in the back of the school, high-jumped, played basketball until I fouled too many times, tried out for cheerleader in a tight skirt and didn't make it. I acted my heart out in the school dramas (Richard has to forgive me for my miserable Lady Macbeth). All the while I read voraciously, studied hard. At Newman I felt I didn't have another choice. Mrs. Schultz and the teachers, they were counting on me.

Mr. Aker encouraged my writing and deplored my grammar. It was in his class that I discovered the joy of fiction writing. Marcelle Peret unleashed my love of painting, which I

110

have rediscovered in the past ten years. The laws of chemistry eluded me, but I shall never forget the patience and humor with which my teacher dealt with my obtuseness. Rowena Pennock was like a formidable boulder which the math deficient had to climb over to get to the next grade. I made it with very skinned knees. Parsing sentences: how boring then, but how useful now that I write. (Why isn't grammar taught anymore?) Mrs. Fredericks's French class was a highlight. She threw us in a sea of French — no English life-preserving words allowed. We even changed identities, becoming Madeleine, Jacques, Marie, Emile, and she gently coached us up to the surface, taught us the right strokes. My greatest regret at Newman was missing Mrs. Grout's senior English class. The word down the halls was that she was a terror, but that she taught you to read with your brain. I could still use that lesson.

I missed out on the excitement of senior year, when the whole class found itself on a new diving board, ready or not for another plunge into an unknown future. Even if I did miss out (my father was transferred to Boston and Mrs. Schultz had me graduate early), I knew I was now a good swimmer thanks to all those hands that had held me while I floundered. But if I'd been able to stay one more year at Newman, I would have been a better one.

*Newman students in front of the Jefferson Building, 1956.*

*Cheerleaders, late 1950s.*

# CHAPTER SEVEN

# One Last Breath of Innocence

—⦁⦁⦁—

*Newman was more than the school you went to. It was a total way of life.*

RICHARD STONE '60

IN THE LATE FIFTIES, to the tune of easy songs such as "Mr. Sandman," the country enjoyed post-war prosperity and the proud pursuit of the suburban American dream. Preserving that pretty picture was a priority, and as the Cold War divided the world, the United States adopted a policy of "containment" to stop the spread of Communism. After Republican Senator Joseph McCarthy accused high-ranking government officials of being Soviet loyalists, Americans began to see Communists every-where. Colleagues and neighbors were rounded up and questioned; careers were ruined, friend-ships shattered.

The "Red Scare" even touched Newman. In 1956, an assistant librarian left the school, and New Orleans, after she and her husband refused to answer questions before U.S. Senate investigators about their alleged Communist activities. "Of course people were horrified," said Richard Stone '60. "She may have been a Communist, but she never bothered the kids. I went down to her husband's travel agency some, and I can assure you no one ever tried to indoc-trinate me."

Wild rumors circulated the school in the wake of the revelations about the librarian. "I had a teacher who was the worst teacher ever, but he wasn't a teacher at all," said Camilla Trinchieri '60. "He was CIA! He was good

*LEFT: Upper School faculty, 1966.*

looking and he used to flirt. He really didn't know what he was doing, because he was there to investigate the librarian. Then they both disappeared." Louis Fishman '59 also remembers this "teacher," but he remembers him as an agent with the Federal Bureau of Investigation. "Those were good people," he said of the librarian and her family. Their daughter was a Newman student about Mr. Fishman's age when the parents were accused.

This was one of the rare instances when the real world intruded on Jefferson Avenue. The life of a typical Newman student revolved around football and basketball games, Homecoming and homework. When they weren't studying, students focused on being cheerleaders, basketball stars, Homecoming queens and leads in the operetta. Many things remained traditional and old-fashioned. Moms still packed lunches such as fried chicken in waxed paper, or roast beef and matzo for Passover. Girls wore full skirts, girdles and high heels, and the old rules of etiquette were strongly enforced. Girls were required to respond in a formal letter to the annual banquet honoring the Girls' Athletic Committee. Ms. Trinchieri remembers jitterbugging in party dresses and panty hose, and "no smooching until much later." Faith U. Fogle '63 remembers getting in trouble because of what she wrote in a journal during her class trip to Washington, D.C. Ralph Kelley, nicknamed "Froggy," had assigned the students to keep journals. And he had required the girls to wear high heels on the trip. "We did nothing but walk," Miss Fogle said. "So I complained in my diary because I had to get up early and put on my high heels and my girdle. I said I'd never be a Supreme Court justice because I had to waste so much time putting on all this stuff."

Mischief was fairly harmless; some students were sent home from a trip to New York City for flying a paper airplane — lit on fire — out the hotel window. Jack Weiss '64, who would

go on to be president of the student council, a fifteen-year Newman trustee and an attorney for *The Wall Street Journal*, was sent home for taking a taxi to get a chocolate ice cream soda. "We were awful," said Bob Lane '64. "We might have been the only class to get to go to New York." Susan Haspel Lipsey '63 said she and her boyfriend were chastised for leaving a concert during the Washington trip. They were apprehended in the lobby, holding hands. Alan Philipson '56, who would go on to be chairman of Newman's Board of Governors, was suspended just before graduation for playing pinball for money at a bar on Danneel Street called Doc's. "Ralph Kelley had been trying to catch us for years," he said. "The proprietor used to stand watch and tell us when he was coming, but she went to the bathroom once, and that's when he came in. He saw us and just turned around and stormed out."

In 1960, just days before graduation, a few wily seniors pulled off a stunning prank. They obtained a key to Newman and snuck into the library and turned every single book around so that the pages, not the spines, now faced front. "It blew the librarian's mind," said Angus Lind '62.

"They intended to leave a very funny message, and it shouldn't have taken very long to fix," said Richard Stone. "But the librarian got hysterical and thought they were rearranged. The administration was horrified. It was as though somebody had been beaten or a bomb had gone off."

A new decade dawned, and John F. Kennedy was sworn in as the thirty-fifth president. Jimmie Davis replaced Earl K. Long in the governor's mansion. Chep Morrison was mayor of New Orleans until 1961, when he resigned to become ambassador to the Organization of American States. The City Council appointed Victor Schiro to finish out his term. Around the same

*Part of the Homecoming Court, 1960, Class of 1961.*

time, the New Orleans Civic Center was completed, and Galatoire's had a $75,000 fire. The Berlin Wall divided East and West Germany in 1961, astronauts from the former Soviet Union and the United States were hurtling into space and NASA built the Michoud Assembly Facility in New Orleans to assemble the Saturn booster rockets used in the Apollo flights to the moon. Americans owned eighty-five million TVs, and movies such as *Ben Hur*, *Psycho* and *Dr. No* were new releases.

Although the United States was on the cusp of swift and dramatic changes in the early 1960s, Newman was enjoying a few more precious, protected years of blissful ignorance. "Things were very tough in New Orleans throughout the sixties," said Lynda Friedmann '66. "But at Newman, we were completely focused on popcorn on the floor of study hall and things like that. We were oblivious."

"We went to Newman in the old era," agreed Harvey Stone '62. "In terms of what you studied, it was all the old-fashioned stuff. Literature was read as literature without any political slants entering in. Christopher Columbus was regarded as the courageous discoverer of America, not as a colonialist oppressor."

In the early years of the new decade, Newman began a new tradition — routinely winning athletic championships, thanks to two new coaches, Ed "Skeets" Tuohy and Tony Reginelli. The Greenies played a perfect football season in 1960 and won the Riverside title. In 1961, the boys played a perfect season in basketball and went on to win the state championship. They won again in 1963 and 1964. Boys and girls won several state swimming championships.

There was a building fundraising drive in 1960 that set an ambitious goal of raising $750,000. By 1962, the campaign had raised $650,000, which at the time was the largest amount ever raised by a local elementary or secondary school. There was

enough money for a new Upper School classroom building — named for former board Chairman Louis Lemle — a conference room and a 500-seat auditorium named for Clarence Henson. There were new science labs and a tree house for Greentrees, and the library moved to the old assembly hall, where it is today. It needed more space: it had grown from 4,000 volumes in 1946 to almost 18,000 in 1963.

In other "news," junior and senior homerooms became coed. "For those students who feel charming, bright and cheerful at 8:30 in the morning, the new situation is ideal," the *Pioneer* reported. "It provides an extra opportunity for contact with the opposite sex." But this was the minority. Most girls said they hated to be seen by boys so early, and they didn't like their conversations about makeup and shoes being overheard. Boys disliked having to keep their topics "suitable for mixed company," the *Pioneer* reported.

Tuition in 1962–63 ranged from $480 to $820. An orthodontist came to school to adjust braces, and the nurse's favorite "medicine" was red-and-white striped peppermints. The Jefferson Building, now sixty years old, was beginning to seem quaint. "I remember the creaky floors and the wooden wainscoting," said Bob Lane. "There was something comforting about it even then." The cafeteria made homemade yeast rolls every day; alumni remember the smell emanating from the kitchen every morning at ten. In fourth grade, the children learned how to write cursive. "If you got it right, you could have a fountain pen," said Genie Everett McCloskey '65. "It was very important to have a fountain pen. You could buy them at a sweet shop at the corner of Jefferson and Loyola. My first one was pink." The Sophomore Bazaar, begun in 1951, had become an established tradition in the 1960s. The fundraising event often had a theme, such as the Wild West.

*Newman's cafeteria in the late 1950s.*

Homecoming was a central event in the life of Newman high-schoolers. Senior lettermen picked the Homecoming Court until the 1970s, when it became more democratic. The queen, elected by the Upper School, was announced at the Friday pep rally, and she sat on an elaborate throne on stage in the Henson Auditorium. Games were played across the river at Behrman Stadium until 1985. The court would travel together in a motorcade of teachers' convertibles. The queen was crowned at half-time by the student council president, and she often hosted a post-game party. Saturday night, there was a semi-formal dance, where, in the sixties, they twisted and jitter-bugged to Chubby Checker and the Shirelles.

Socializing included "lots of time in somebody's car," said Harvey Stone. "I lived six short blocks from school but I would drive a car there, even though I would have to park a block and a half away." The popular hangouts will sound familiar: Bruno's, the Camellia Grill and the Napoleon House in the French Quarter. "Clarence 'Frogman' Henry was always playing some-where in the Quarter," Mr. Stone said. "And you could walk into Preservation Hall with no problem. There was no line." Cards, pool and pinball were the rage among the boys.

A few favorite teachers from an earlier era remained at Newman in the late fifties and early sixties, most notably Mrs. Grout and, until 1962, Mr. Frederick. "Wayne Frederick was the greatest educator I ever met — from kindergarten through Harvard Law School," said Richard Stone. "He had an incredible ability to differentiate among people who were very good in the context of high school and those whose talent was going to take them far in life." Take Michael Devlin '60, now a well-known opera singer. "I thought he was a bum," Mr. Stone said of his childhood friend. "But Mr. Frederick knew he would be famous."

Mr. Stone knew a softer side of the terrifying English teacher, Mrs. Grout: "She was terrific companionship — inter-esting, open and warm. I used to have lunch with her every time I came to New Orleans. She loved a martini or a Manhattan and a good lunch."

Angus Lind '62, a columnist for the *Times-Picayune*, also had occasional contact with Mrs. Grout long after he left Newman:

> *I can remember at least on two occasions I got my column clipped out and sent to me in the mail with a note from Mrs. Grout basically saying, "Dear Angus, Enjoyed your column Sunday. Very informative. However in the third paragraph, your misuse of the participle . . ." And she's got marks, like she's grading! I mean this is thirty years later and this woman is grading my column.*

It did not take long for Frank Cernicek, who began teaching history and geography in the mid-1950s, to become a Newman legend. Two years after the librarian was accused of "un-American activities," Mr. Cernicek, who escaped Czechoslovakia during World War II, made news by doing something quintessentially American: he became a citizen. The ceremony was featured in the November 6, 1958, *New Orleans States, New Orleans Item*:

> *Frank Cernicek had his finest hour yesterday afternoon.*
>
> *If the tall, blond, crew-cut, handsome native of Czechoslovakia valiantly tried to hide that lump in his throat, if he brushed away a "speck of dust" from his eyes, those in the crowded courtroom of federal Judge Skelly Wright pretended not to notice.*

*Frank Cernicek, history and geography teacher from 1955–1987.*

The article goes on to note the large crowd of teens in the courtroom, an unusual sight at a naturalization ceremony. They were members of Mr. Cernicek's classes. "It was very moving," said Angus Lind, who was there. Ninety-two students came in two busloads with Mr. Kelley, whom Jack Weiss described as the teacher who continually found ways to give his students real-life civics lessons. Mr. Cernicek told the newspaper he was overwhelmed by the experience and was looking forward to the first opportunity he would have to vote. Frank Cernicek's parents left his native country and became U.S. citizens before their son was eighteen. He stayed behind to finish his studies, all the while working with the underground when Czechoslovakia was occupied by the Germans during World War II. Mr. Cernicek came west via Canada, and then traveled to New York on a student visa to attend Columbia University. He received a master's degree in political science, and moved with his wife, also Czech, to New Orleans.

After the naturalization ceremony, Mr. Cernicek's students gave him an alligator wallet. Miss Devlin presented him with one of her trademark scrolls, dedicated to "Uncle Frank, Citizen of the Year." All his students had signed it.

Alumni remember Mr. Cernicek as knowledgeable, passionate and challenging. "He was the first teacher that really put demands on me and ooh, was he tough," said Darryl Berger '65. "And he had a thousand stories to tell. He'd been wounded and he walked with a limp. We'd prod him to tell us how he fought the Nazis."

"He had a passion for American history because this was his adopted country," Mr. Lane said. Mr. Lind said he did things no teacher would get away with today. "If you dozed off in his class he'd rap you on the head," he said. "And if you got your Indian tribes mixed up, he'd threaten you with another." Billy Conway '75 remembers him hurling chalk at miscreants. He would say, "Buddy Boy, I am going to teach you a lesson."

Rowena Pennock "was the epitome of the old school marm," Mr. Lind said. "If you said one word out of order, you were looking at detention. But she had a knack for teaching." Alan Philipson said Mrs. Pennock would rap students' knuckles with a yardstick. "We learned the hard way, but no one complained, and we all came out better for it," he said. Mrs. Pennock was also known for her insistence on precise logic. She was fond of saying, "See that white house across the street? I don't live there."

Julia Meyer Bromley '63 remembers Ralph Slifkin not so much for his teaching, but for his singing. "He was a cantor at Touro," she said. "We all swooned over him. And on high holy days, we'd go to Touro, just to hear him sing. He was wonderful. Once the school would not let us out when it snowed, but he did. And he taught us all about snowflakes."

Evelyn Landis was a favorite in the English department. "She was so dear," Mr. Berger said. "She was very sensitive to kids' feelings. She was like a favorite great aunt." Harry Blumenthal '63, who was chairman of the Board of Governors from 1998 to 2000, called her "an all-time favorite. She was a great role model and she instilled an enthusiasm for learning in all her students." Mrs. McCloskey said she was "always positive and supportive. And if you saw her today, she looks just the way she always did — slim with beautiful silver-gray hair."

The beginning of the end of innocence came on November 21, 1963, the day President Kennedy was assassinated in Dallas, Texas. Newman students remember the day with vivid precision. "I was in Mrs. (Rae) Leuthner's third-grade classroom," said Karen Scharff Alvarez '73. "We were waiting for her to come into the class. And when she did walk in, she was crying and explained to us that Kennedy had been shot. I've always thought that the seriousness of this event was made apparent to me because it was the first time, and probably the only time, I have seen a teacher cry." Cathy Norman Penland '73 said she remembers how traumatic it was to see her parents crying. She also remembers her teacher crying; her class was given colored pencils and paper to occupy them while the teachers huddled together to mourn. Many students remember crowding into the nurse's office or the student lounge to listen to the latest news on the radio or watch it on TV. "It was the first of that type of tragedy," said Linda Gottesman Baum '67. "It wasn't commonplace for horrible things to happen."

Jack Weiss said that as he listened to the news in the senior room, he felt life as he had known it was ending. "I really identified with him, and life was never the same after that," he said. Lou Good '71 was unnerved by some children in his class who were happy the president was dead. "They were going around spreading the good news," he recalled. "It was terrible." Mrs. Shultz called the school together in an assembly and then dismissed everyone early. The November 27 issue of the *Greenie* was printed in black ink instead of green, and the cover con-

*CLOCKWISE FROM TOP LEFT: Evelyn Landis, English teacher in the 1950s and 1960s. William Cunningham, Newman's headmaster from 1964 to 1976. A portrait of Anvilla Shultz, head of the Upper School and college counselor from 1953 until 1975. Angela Devlin, art teacher and head of the Lower School, 1930 to 1972. Rae Leuthner, third-grade teacher from 1951 to 1964.*

*Class of 1958, in their junior year.*

sisted only of a quote from U.S. Senator Mike Mansfield: "A piece of each of us died at that moment. Yet in death he gave of himself to us . . . He gave each of us of his love that we, too, in turn, might give."

In 1964, the year the streetcars stopped running on Canal Street, the conflict in Vietnam began to escalate into a war and claim American lives. It was also when Principal Eddy Kalin retired. His departure, after decades at the school, was marked with parties and speeches, and, of course, an epic poem penned by Miss Devlin.

His replacement, William Cunningham, was the first director of the school to be called a "headmaster." Raised in the suburbs of New York, he held a B.A. from Wesleyan University and a master's degree in secondary education from Northwestern University. He had been an assistant principal and chairman of the history department at the Kinkaid School in Houston, as well as a headmaster at a school in Menlo Park, California. He was squarely built and tall — six feet two inches — and arrived at Newman with a flattop haircut and a wife name Mildred, or Mid. They had two sons, Bruce '70 and Scott '69, and they lived next door to Newman in a house that later was razed to make way for the science center.

*Class of 1970 in Lower School.*

Mr. Cunningham had two veteran administrators on hand to help him acclimate — Anvilla Shultz and Angela Devlin. Everyone fondly remembers Mrs. Shultz, principal of the Upper School as well as the college guidance counselor from the mid-1950s until 1975. Much like the college counselors of today, she worked tirelessly to match each student's need and potential with the right college or university. In assembly speeches and in individual meetings, she hammered into students the importance of getting into a good college. Mrs. Shultz was from Springfield, Massachusetts and had a master's degree from Columbia. After finishing graduate school, she became the assistant dean of women at Allegheny College in Pennsylvania. She came to New Orleans in 1951 after she married, and taught history at Metairie Park Country Day School before coming to Newman in 1953. "She was a great figure in the history of the school," said Jack Weiss. "She personified academic excellence. She was a person of unquestionable academic substance who had extraordinary educational ideals, and who had the complete respect of the faculty."

When Mrs. Shultz retired, the *Newman News* said:

*An era of loveliness has ended at Newman. The most gracious of ladies, the essence of femininity, the most gentle heart has retired. Her ears were open to problems large and small. The troubled and restless found within her an honest friend. She has helped to bring Newman to the position that it holds today. She has influenced the education which the school provides and has impressed the faculty, administration and graduates with the ideals Newman promotes.*

Miss Devlin, a graduate of Newcomb Art School and Columbia, began at Newman in 1930 as art teacher and was head of the Lower School for decades before retiring in 1972.

She was old-fashioned and feminine, and wore her hair in tight, neat curls at the nape of her neck. She was famous around Newman for the epic poems she would write for special occasions. She summed up her philosophy on Lower School education in 1954: "I think we demand too little of young people in an intellectual way. Children and young people are often capable of more than we ask of them."

In May 1968, Mr. Cunningham made a short announcement during an assembly in the Henson Auditorium: the following fall, Newman would become an integrated school. It was reported in a *Greenie* editorial entitled: "An Easy Transition — Hopefully:"

*With racial integration of Newman becoming a reality next fall, we feel the greatest mistake the administration can make in accommodating Negro students is to draw too much attention to them.*

*In the past, Newman students have, on the whole, reacted maturely and wisely to changes in school policy. They have the ability and background to accept the Negro children as fellow students without any difficulty.*

*If the administration, however, draws too much attention to this adjustment, students may become self-conscious and a natural and casual change will become impossible.*

*We feel that Mr. Cunningham's one announcement of the integration policy is sufficient.*

RIGHT: *Newman class of 1965 and teacher Ralph Kelley in Attorney General Robert Kennedy's office in Washington, D.C., 1962.*

# GREENTREES

*BY WALTER ISAACSON '70*

*Walter Isaacson, one of today's leading journalists, was destined for greatness even at Newman: he was voted most likely to succeed. After graduating from Harvard, he was named a Rhodes Scholar and attended Pembroke College of Oxford. His first reporting jobs were with* The Sunday Times of London *and* The New Orleans States-Item/Times-Picayune. *He joined* Time *in 1978 as a national affairs writer in New York, and then moved to Washington as a political correspondent. In 1995, he was named managing editor. In 2001, he was named chairman and CEO of CNN, overseeing the cable channel's news shows, including those for radio and in airports. In January 2003, the Aspen Institute, an international non-profit organization studying global issues, named Mr. Isaacson President and CEO. He is the author of several books, including* Kissinger: A Biography, *and* Benjamin Franklin: An American Life.

MY MOST VIVID AND VITAL MEMORY from Newman is, of course, of Greentrees, and not merely because I have reached that stage of life when my most vivid and vital memories are my earliest ones. It was no more than a tiny grove near the old Stern Building, but to our even tinier eyes it was an enchanted forest. "Once upon a time Newman children played under a stand of beautiful trees near this spot," reads the apolo-getic plaque on the bookstore building that replaced our ver-dant temple. Sometimes I go back and touch the plaque to see if it still nurtures the embers of nostalgia from what it sheepishly calls "that special time and place."

*Vilma Bingham Dulany, bookstore manager from 1963 to 1992, stands by the plaque at the entrance to the bookstore, which is located where the old playground once was.*

Although we did not know it then, Greentrees contained more lessons than all the classrooms of all the teachers we would have over thirteen years, no matter how great each and every Miss LaFrantz and Mrs. Grout turned out to be. It was the first place where we were permitted to venture out on our own, and there we learned to be little explorers in a world teeming with wonders yet still enveloped in security. To paraphrase that Robert Fulghum book of a few years back, which highlighted these lessons of kindergarten, almost all we really needed to know we could learn in Greentrees.

There were plants large and small, each struggling to reach the sun, and even some that we had sowed ourselves in plastic trays on a window sill and then transplanted into the worm-rich soil. And we learned that as they grew taller their roots grew equally deeper, and that both processes were just as important to their well-being, the growing up and the deepening of roots in the ground of Greentrees.

There were also the inchworms. They, too, seemed always heading upward. Hunching their backs, then extending themselves, they would bend and stretch and reach for the sky, inch by inch, as they made their mysterious pilgrimage up the bark of the trees. And if and when something happened and they fell to the ground, they would resume their journey unfazed, along the same path, inch by inch.

There were very few rules, but they were important ones. Find a buddy. Take turns. Clean up any mess you make. No whining. Those turned out to be important for the real world as well. We also learned another lesson there, and I can still hear its sing-song chant: Sticks and stones will break your bones but words will never hurt you. That one turned out to be wrong, as we would later discover, but it was useful to learn that not every lesson turns out to be right.

And there were Justin and Robby and Steffi and Billy and Alan and Allan and Chip and Chaffe and at least two Lindas, each with their own lessons to teach. When it was time to leave each day, we would all gather under the metal and plastic

*Benny Brown, a Newman janitor.*

awning on Loyola Street to wait for our carpools, and the kindly old janitor would help us into the car and we would remember to say, "Thank you, Brown," until Billy's father, who was a rabbi, taught us another little lesson, and thenceforth we would remember to call him "Mr. Brown."

Eventually we learned the lifelong lessons — hold hands, look both ways — that allowed us to cross the street to Ferro's Food Store and, figuring out the value of a dime and a dollar, buy a Barq's or, in those days before Doritos, a bag of Lay's barbecued chips. And once we had learned to read, we could look at the sign in the window of the Laundromat on Jefferson Avenue that said "whites only" and learn to wonder why.

Even after we became third graders, and thus very sophisticated, we would still go back to Greentrees occasionally. And being by then a bit more mischievous, we would sometimes knock the inchworms off the trees and onto the ground. But they would still resume their journey to their mysterious high destinations, inch by inch by inch.

Even today I sometimes yearn to go back to Greentrees where we spent such wondrous days, in the words of James Agee, so successfully disguised to ourselves as children. But Greentrees exists now only in memory, and I guess that may be its final lesson for us. Nothing ever remains the same, except a few timeless lessons that are as valid in Act III as they were in Act I. Remember the roots. Remember the inchworms. And because there are still a few streets left to cross, remember to hold hands.

*Detail, mural by Tony Green: theater at Newman.*

# CHAPTER EIGHT

# New Faces

*The key at Newman was to be something, something in particular. I was the black kid who did theater. I was sort of a star like that, and very accepted.*

LEO JONES '73

GERALD WILLIAMS, Reginald Jackson and Leo Jones were like most Newman students — bright, enthusiastic and talented. One had natural leadership and athletic abilities; one had an unusually high I.Q. and a beautiful voice, and one was a gifted thespian. When they walked into Newman in September 1968, they were strangers in a strange land, and they had no idea what to expect. Neither did Newman. They were the first black students to attend Isidore Newman School; in fact, they were the first black students to attend any private, non-parochial school in the New Orleans area. It was a quietly momentous day in the history of the school, and in the history of race relations in New Orleans.

Race relations have always been a little different in New Orleans than in the rest of the South. For various reasons, desegregation was, on the whole, peaceful here — except when it came to the public schools. It was in front of the schoolhouse doors that battle lines were drawn and neighbors turned on neighbors.

In 1960, under pressure from influential New Orleanians passionately opposed to integration, the state legislature tried to close the city's schools rather than allow desegregation. Governor Jimmie Davis, known as the "singing governor" who penned the hit song, "You are my Sunshine," tried to take over the New

LEFT: *Cast of* Bye Bye Birdie, *spring of 1973.*

*A segregated Laundromat near Newman in the 1960s.*

Orleans schools to preserve segregation. A series of court battles resulted in four lone girls integrating two public schools — which had virtually emptied of white children in advance of their arrival. They faced ugly and sometimes violent protest. There were only four black students because the school board created a "pupil placement law" — later ruled illegal — with so many restrictions that most blacks did not qualify for the white schools. In 1961, a total of six schools were integrated with twelve black students. That year, the Catholic schools desegregated. In 1966, Fifth Circuit Court of Appeals Judge John Minor Wisdom, a Newman graduate and a passionate supporter of desegregation, handed down a decision that effectively ended the practice of token integration. In the coming years, white flight to the suburbs increased dramatically. By 1968, more than half the students in the New Orleans public schools were black.

Of course, discrimination and separation of the races persisted. Newman coach Bradley Farris '73 remembers a Laundromat near Newman with a sign that said, "White only. Maids in uniform accepted." In 1962, when the University of Mississippi was integrated, history teacher Ken MacKenzie recalled having some "lively discussions" with his students, some of whom were ardent segregationists. Nationwide in the sixties, while the courts had effectively ended some segregation, the civil rights movement was becoming increasingly violent. Sit-ins, marches and boycotts often turned bloody as segregationists fought to hold on to the old ways. When Martin Luther King Jr. was assassinated in 1967, Newman had to cancel the annual trip to Washington because of unrest there.

It is no surprise, then, that private schools, which had a choice, were hesitant to integrate. In fact, it would be several years after Newman began recruiting blacks before any other private, non-parochial school followed suit. The decision to allow — and even recruit — black students, required intense discussion among trustees. Herman Kohlmeyer Jr. '49 and a few other young trustees led the charge. "A bunch of young guys, me and four or five others, went to the old-timers on the board and said, 'Look, we think we ought to do this,'" said Mr. Kohlmeyer. Some board members worried the school would become a target for segregationists, or that the black students would feel isolated. But the board liked the idea of being the first private school to open its doors to blacks. It was in keeping with the inclusive principles on which the school was founded. Looking back on the process of bringing blacks into Newman, Mr. Kohlmeyer said, "It was the most important thing that happened in my thirty years on the board."

*RIGHT: Members of the class of 1974 when they were in the Lower School.*

For Gerald Williams, Reginald Jackson and Leo Jones, making it at Newman was probably a lot more important than making history. Mr. Williams was only five years old when he entered Newman, so everyone in his class was new to the school. Mr. Jackson entered the seventh grade and Mr. Jones joined the eighth grade class, so they faced the challenge of fitting into a group that had known each other since kindergarten. Mr. Jackson left after a few years to attend a northeastern boarding school. Mr. Williams '81 said that overall, "It was a positive experience in terms of long-term relationships and from the standpoint of academics, for preparing me for what was down the road." As for being black at Newman, he said, "I didn't know any different. I made friends and I did sleepovers and all that. I was very sheltered, actually, until I left. I caught some grief from other teams who would notice I was the only black on our team — a lot of opposing teams were all black — but that's it." Mr. Williams was a leader — athletically, academically and socially. "I didn't give anyone much ammunition." He did say he worked a little harder, to prove he was "worthy" of being there. And, he said, he "caught a little grief" back home, in his neighborhood, from kids who said he "talked funny" or "didn't sound black."

Mr. Jones '73 was old enough to know that his arrival at Newman was meaningful:

> *It was a big deal. I felt like school integration was something you saw movies about. I didn't know anyone who'd integrated a school. But this was a private school, so it felt a lot less formal. People weren't going to pay any attention to how smoothly it went. And it was basically really softer than I thought it was going to be. There wasn't a lot of overt ugliness. And a lot of people were exceptionally nice.*

Like Mr. Williams, Mr. Jones had a niche, a talent: he was an actor. Everyone remembers him as Christopher Robin in *Winnie the Pooh* and Conrad in *Bye Bye Birdie* "He was the undisputed king of drama," said Mark Amoss '73. "Nobody ever gave Leo a hard time."

Mr. Jones agreed:

> *Doing* Bye Bye Birdie *underscored the way things went for me at Newman. I didn't think I would not receive a role, or anything, purely because I was a black student. I assumed if I was the best person for the part, I was going to get it. I remember there was a guy who sure did look a lot more the part than I did, but I was sure I would get it, and I did! That says a lot for the people who were in charge of the drama program. And when we did* Winnie the Pooh, *I played Christopher Robin. They weren't looking for some white kid with blond hair; I played it.*

The only time he felt the school treated him differently was when Mrs. Shultz suggested to his mother that he attend a black college. She said he had endured so much isolation at Newman that it might be nice to be at a school where he was invited to parties. Mr. Jones was shocked. "I said, 'Oh, there are parties I don't get invited to?' It never crossed my mind there was something I wasn't in on. I had a complete social life outside of Newman. I went to dances at McDonough 35 and Fortier, because I liked their music better."

Being among the first black students at a school such as Newman presented challenges, even for kids who seemed to thrive there. In 1974, David Sylvester '74 wrote an essay called "A Black Perspective" for the *Greenie* about his five years at Newman:

*"Swearing in of President John F. Kennedy" as portrayed by members of the class of 1973 in Kindergarten.*

*It would be more than ridiculous to say that being black at Newman is a bed of roses. One of the biggest hassles I've come across is being aware that the people around me are trying to be totally conscious of what they're saying in an effort not to offend me. This, however, offends me almost as much as anything they could've said, because what I see the person doing is bringing out the differences between us.*

*However, the biggest problem I've faced here is looking up in class and becoming deeply aware that no matter how many people are in the room, I am alone and really have no one to identify with.*

*I've met some fantastic folks who have meant a lot to me. Besides receiving the best education in the city, I've learned a lot of things, and hopefully taught some folks that people can't and shouldn't be classified.*

*There have also been some great experiences, too numerous to really go into, except for one. Once while playing basketball, the guy that was guarding me called me a "dirty Jew."*

Today, Mr. Sylvester has a softer view of his Newman years:

*We could never have afforded Newman — I went on scholarship. It was the first time I had such a large exposure to white folks. It was quite a culture shock. People had way more privilege than I ever thought was possible. But it went fine. I made lots of friends. There were a lot of families that made my transition unbelievably positive. Lots of people said, "This kid is just a kid." Dating was the toughest. I didn't even ask. Now I talk to people and they say, "Why didn't you ask?" I think a lot of the loneliness and isolation came from inside me.*

While some alumni hardly remember integration, others say it was the defining event of their Newman experience. "It was the number one most significant thing that happened," said Bill Hines '74.

*There really was an incredible level of ignorance and fear — it was mostly the parents, but it was passed on to the students. Even if you were a nice person, you wondered, "What will it do to the school?" and "Will they be different?" No one knew any African-Americans socially. And suddenly, you have African-American kids coming over to play. That was a sea change. It took time for everyone to become friendly. Even having lunch with a black person was new to us, at thirteen years old. So what? So, nothing. That's what we found out. There was no real difference.*

"I think Newman was accepting of black students, but there were so few," said Cathy Norman Penland '73. "But I know of at least one family that pulled their kids out of school when integration took place." Bryan Batt '81 knew of parents who would not let black students sleep over at their houses.

But Billy Conway '75 said he didn't remember any controversy. "No one was whispering about it. That is not to say you would have found uniform attitudes of acceptance of black people. Probably a large minority carried around racial prejudice, but it never came up."

As blacks began to enter Newman, English teacher David Bain offered a black history course in which he vowed to "tell it like it is." It was an informal course with no grades or tests.

By the early seventies, most private schools had dropped their whites-only policies, because the federal government had withdrawn tax-exempt status for schools that held onto them.

But as late as 1972, Newman remained the only private non-parochial K-12 school in New Orleans that actually had black students.

Integration was just one of the many ways Newman was changing in the late sixties and early seventies. Students were becoming more vocal in their criticism of the school, and less afraid to question authority. They complained about school policy in the *Greenie*, and pushed for changes in the curriculum. And they were becoming more aware of the world around them: they worried about pollution in Lake Pontchartrain, the declining New Orleans economy and the increase in sub-standard housing. They organized an interschool group, funded by the Stern family, called Urban Studies in Action, to study the city's issues. In 1969, Newman students begin tutoring about a dozen children from McDonough 14 and Allen public schools. The project was organized by students Tommy Friedmann '70 and Walter Isaacson '70; the faculty advisor was Mr. Bain, who brought in two students from Tulane's School of Social Work to conduct sensitivity training for the tutors.

Former board Chairman Jay Lapeyre '71 said Vietnam was a "huge issue" for his class. "Thinkers and smart people were anti-war and athletes tended to support the war. It was a very polarizing time. You were an athlete or you weren't. You were for the war or against it. You did drugs or you did not."

Bill Hines remembers the fear of draft numbers. "I was one of the last classes that got draft numbers," he said. "The possibility of getting drafted was very much on your mind. There were kids ahead of me who went to Vietnam."

History teacher Ken MacKenzie spent a lot of time in his classes discussing Vietnam and whether the United States should be there. "The students were very divided," he said.

Mark Amoss remembers Newman as a school dealing with a lot of the social issues of the day, but in a microscopic way:

*And the administration was very conservative. It had a somewhat unbending view of how students should behave. You could never wear jeans. Teddy Cotonio, who was an English teacher at the time, told us it was laughable that the children who were one day going to be the leaders of the city would be aching to wear what he viewed as proletariat garb. That was a tough act to sell to kids being bombarded with the anti-establishment rhetoric of the day.*

As the sixties became the seventies, Newman abandoned its dress code and simply stated that students could not wear jeans, shorts or "skooter skirts," a popular style of miniskirt. The new rules were dubbed the "un-dress code" by the students. It was received enthusiastically by the students, if less so by the teachers. "We spent a lot of time playing cops and robbers on the dress code," Mr. MacKenzie said. By 1971, boys were sporting long hair and sideburns, and girls were enjoying sanctioned miniskirts and pants. Valerie Besthoff Marcus '78 recalls that when pants were first allowed for girls at Newman, it was required that they wear a long tunic over them, to cover their rear ends. "And you still couldn't wear jeans when I graduated in 1978," she said.

The Beatles, who played in City Park in 1964, were all the rage. One year, the Newman Dads Club sponsored a "Beatles Concert" in the auditorium. The kids screamed, the dads wore wigs and they lip-synced "I wanna hold your hand." "Everyone was screaming and loving it and in the middle of it all I realized that one of those dads up there was MY DAD and I was horrified!" said Karen Scharff Alvarez '73.

By 1968, the administration saw the need for a doctor to

come and speak to the Upper School about the dangers of drugs. A 1970 survey found that twelve percent of Newman students had tried an illegal drug, and in most cases it was marijuana. Smoking did not become taboo until the 1970s — in the sixties, the *Greenie* printed editorials complaining that students should be allowed to smoke at school, to avoid having "nicotine fits" in the middle of class.

The social divisions between Jewish and non-Jewish students were fading in the late sixties, thanks in part to the elimination of high school sororities and fraternities. "That was pretty much in the background by the time we came along," Mr. Amoss said. As a non-Jew, he found the Judaic traditions of his classmates very interesting, and he has maintained a lifelong interest in Judaism and in the Holocaust, thanks to his exposure to Jewish children at Newman. Cathy Usdin Burka '68 said she was one of the first Jewish girls to be admitted to the Valencia Club. "I was of the generation where things were changing for Jewish people in New Orleans," she said. Of course, some divisions remained. Michael Lewis '78 remembers that the Squires, his teenage Carnival group, did not accept Jews. "I questioned my dad about it — it seemed so absurd," he said.

In 1968, the yearbook debuted, taking the place of the final issue of the *Pioneer*. It was named *Absinthe* after the potent and toxic spirit that was banned in the United States in the early twentieth century. The students' reasoning was that absinthe is green and spirited, like Newman. It's not clear what the administration was thinking.

In 1968, Newman kicked off the "Campaign for Excellence," a $750,000 capital improvement campaign. It funded renovations to the Jefferson Building, the conversion of the Valmont Building into the Middle School, a library renovation, and the construction of the two-story Heymann Science Center.

"The building will be virtually windowless," the *Greenie* reported. "The exterior will be textured stucco to give the building the ultra modern look." All of the improvements, completed in 1970, cost $1 million. A darkroom in the new science center inspired students to form a photography club. Many new clubs appeared in the early seventies, including those for scuba diving, sailing, folk music and waterskiing.

By 1969, the year Neil Armstrong walked on the moon and the New Orleans Jazz & Heritage Festival debuted in Congo Square, Newman was made up of eight buildings, a staff of eighty and 865 students. Tuition ranged from $650 to $1,200. In 1970, Newman began offering a computer class, using a Loyola University computer. Students were taught Kingston FORTRAN II, the language then most commonly used for math and science. Two years later, Newman was sharing a computer with a local business and several schools. Using a PDP-11 made by Digital Equipment, students now learned a new language: "Basic Plus." The course was limited to seniors.

Around 1971, a new mascot made a brief appearance — the great Green Chicken. "The Green Chicken accomplished much in the way of encouraging spirit," the *Absinthe* said. "Although at times, it seemed it was being more laughed at than with." The only evidence of the mascot was a picture in the yearbook of a student holding an actual, raw chicken during an assembly. But the students went so far as to stage an operetta called "Green Chicken — Superbird," before a game against St. Martin's.

In the early seventies, as President Richard Nixon and his administration came under increasing scrutiny for their role in a break-in at the Watergate offices of the Democratic National Committee, the students came up with a new form of student government: a constitutional convention system. Under Mr.

ABSINTHE
1968

ISIDORE NEWMAN SCHOOL
NEW ORLEANS, LOUISIANA

ABSINTHE
1968

*The cover and title page of the first issue of the* Absinthe, *Newman's yearbook. It debuted in 1968.*

MacKenzie's guidance, they formed committees for different aspects of student life. It evolved into the Executive Committee in place today, where students and faculty share responsibility for student government.

Another capital fund drive got underway in the early seventies, this time asking for $800,000, for land, a student center, a new girls' gym, additional Lower School class space and updates to the Stern Building, including air-conditioning. In 1973, construction began on the Bertha Marcus Levy Student Center, the Lower School building at Jefferson and Loyola avenues, and additions to the Stern Building. Despite calls going back more than a decade, the new plans did not include a girls' gym.

Newman teaching legends came and went. Miss Devlin retired in 1972 and Mrs. Shultz in 1975. And there was a horrific tragedy: Herbert Behrend III, a well-loved teacher known as "Big Herb," was murdered in 1971. Fellow science teacher Ralph Weddington and Mr. Cunningham identified his body at the morgue. "It was simply awful," Mr. Weddington said. "Mr. Cunningham and I held hands like children when we went. I can't think of anything worse that I've ever experienced. But Newman really came together for it." A memorial to him in the 1972 *Absinthe* said: "Though possibly the toughest teacher at Newman, he was considered by his students as one of the best."

Bob Pfister tops everyone's list of favorites from the sixties and seventies. "He was the beloved math teacher," Mrs. Burka said. Linda Gottesman Baum '67 said, "He just really, really cared about kids, and he wanted to be sure you understood the math."

"He was almost a cult figure," said Bill Hines. "He had the ability to take kids who were struggling or didn't like math and get them to buy into it and get it. I placed out of math my first year at Princeton. He would jog with kids, or do whatever they liked to do, to help them out and be their friends." Monte Lemann '79 said he participated in the process of learning with the students. "And boy was he a cheerleader," he said. "He went to every game, every performance." Mr. Pfister ran the clock at basketball games and collected tickets at football games.

And he did something that wouldn't exactly endear him to today's parents and administrators. "He used to take us drinking," said Lou Good '71. "There was a Polynesian restaurant at Pontchartrain Beach called Bali Ha'i and he'd take us there." Mrs. Burka remembers him at parties: "He went to parties and drank Hairy Buffaloes — where you mix all the alcohol together in one big vat."

Robert Pfister was a native New Orleanian who graduated from Fortier and Tulane, where he earned a master of science degree. He was in the Navy in the fifties, stationed in Pearl Harbor, where he developed a taste for Mai Tai cocktails. He returned and began teaching at Newman in the mid-fifties and he would stay for his entire career, except for a brief stint in the sixties at Sperry Gyroscope Co. in Great Neck, N.Y., where he designed submarine navigational systems. He was appointed chairman of Newman's math department in 1966. "He was way out smart," said Mr. Good. "Newman was very fortunate to have him."

Everyone seems to have a particular, personal memory of Mr. Pfister. Billy Conway said he would compose couplets about people. Mr. Lemann remembers Mr. Pfister the opera buff. "He collected oodles of recordings, most on reel-to-reel," he said. He left his library to Newman, and Mr. Lemann added to it and turned it into a collection. Mr. Lemann also said his math teacher slept only about four hours a night. "And he had this gorgeous white Jaguar XKE," Mr. Good said. "When it rained, he would leave it in the garage and walk to school rather than get it wet." Mr. Pfister's convertible ferried the Homecoming queen across the river to the big game every fall.

When Bob Pfister died in December 1981 of cancer, there was a memorial service for him in Henson Auditorium and a fund was established in his name. Mr. MacKenzie said of him: "He never saw anything but the good in people, and for him, every student was a special human being who needed to discover his or her own worth."

Mr. MacKenzie began teaching history at Newman in 1962, and retired in 2000. "I came down from Connecticut for a couple years, and stayed," he said. He was known for his strict, almost military style, and he was fond of calling people "Ace" or "People!" or saying, "Good Job Chief!" He could send chills down his students' spines, but he was also known for his distinctive, rolling laugh.

"The only F I ever got in my life was from him," said Stephanie Bruno '70. "He wanted to teach us how to approach problems about history and how to explore them. His big issue was cause and effect."

"He provided probably the best springboard to go from high school to college," said Ken Beer '75. "He taught us how to research a paper, how to study, what to study." Walter Isaacson said in a 1984 speech that as a reporter covering politics, he was tempted many times to dig out the paper he wrote for Mr. MacKenzie comparing Jeffersonian and Jacksonian democracy.

A native of Long Island, New York, Mr. MacKenzie attended Bates College and then Columbia, where he earned a master's degree in history. He authored a textbook: *America*

CLOCKWISE FROM TOP LEFT: *Robert Pfister, math teacher from 1954 until his death in 1981. Kitty Greenberg, drama, Humanities teacher, and assistant to the headmaster, 1971 to the present. H. Davis Prescott, who came to Newman as an English teacher in 1966 and is today Newman's librarian. Ralph Weddington, science teacher, department chairman and alumni relations assistant, 1966 to 2003. Ken MacKenzie, history teacher from 1962 to 2000. Herbert Behrend III, a science teacher who was found murdered in 1971.*

*Challenged: U.S. History 1916–1945.* He said his teaching and grading style was inspired by Mrs. Grout: "I was tough, but they eventually found out I was softer than I came across."

Travis LeBlanc '95 said he took every class Mr. MacKenzie taught. His senior year, he took three of his classes in a row. "There was at least one day when I would be with him all morning," he said. His admiration for his history teacher was so well-known that classmates began calling him "Chief," Mr. MacKenzie's oft-used nickname for students. Barbara Bell Barrett '82 said Mr. MacKenzie's teaching sparked her lifelong love of history. "He taught how history repeats itself and how you can learn from that," she said.

H. Davis Prescott, Newman's librarian, came to Newman in 1966. As soon as he arrived, he was making students smile, and his classroom became a hangout and a haven. "We would all sign out of study hall to go to his room," Mr. Good said. "It was more fun to be with him. He had a bottle of Windex and he was always cleaning desks and windows. He was entertaining — always cleaning up. He was not a disciplinarian. It was just pleasant to be in his room." A native New Orleanian educated at Fortier and Tulane, Mr. Prescott started at Newman as an English teacher. He then taught civics and was the Middle School principal before becoming the librarian in 1976, when Erminia Wadsworth retired. He earned his master's degree in library science from LSU in the early seventies in anticipation of that move. The *Greenie* said in 1973 that Mr. Prescott's door was always open and smelled like cleaning supplies. He was always up "for a lively debate or a quick game of chess."

Mr. Prescott and Mr. Weddington, a chemistry and physics teacher who also came to Newman in 1966, used to lead the trip to Washington together. Mr. Weddington continued traveling to Washington with the ninth-graders for decades. "He had a great teaching style. He was one of our class favorites," Mrs. Penland said.

Nicknamed "Big Wed," he was a teacher and science department chairman who quit teaching in the early nineties to work on alumni relations. Mr. Weddington retired in 2003. He was known for chain smoking and for his thick, dark-framed glasses and in the seventies, he taught students how to brew alcoholic beverages in his lab. He said it helped them learn about the various micro-organisms present in the fermentation process. The *Greenie* reported, "The sight is rather amusing and odor is perfectly definable."

"I was a little on the hammy side," Mr. Weddington admitted. Mr. Weddington believed in making science as pleasant as possible. When he looks back on his years at Newman, he starts naming students who impressed him through the years, such as journalist Walter Isaacson '70 and ethnobotanist and author Mark Plotkin '73. He can name students going back to the sixties, and he knows what they are doing today.

Kitty Greenberg, a Maryland native, arrived in 1971 and reinvigorated the theater program at Newman. "She made drama mainstream," Mr. Amoss said.

> *"She made it something even guys in sports wanted to participate in. She was extremely talented and she had a way with the kids. She knew how to reach out to you and she knew each kid's strengths and weaknesses. She had high expectations but she was always in a good mood. You could sit down and laugh with Kitty."*

Mr. Conway remembers doing very challenging productions with Mrs. Greenberg.

*A scene from Newman's production of* Annie Get Your Gun *in 1980.*

Monte Lemann said Mrs. Greenberg had "great energy. She was very inclusive, and very stimulating, with just enough informality to bring people out." When he was a junior, Bryan Batt, now an accomplished Broadway, movie and television actor, was stopped in the hallway by Mrs. Greenberg, who said, "When are you going to try out for one of my plays? I know you want to."

"When someone stops you and looks into your soul and reads you like *The New York Times*, and with authority, you listen," Mr. Batt said.

As for Mrs. Greenberg, who is today the assistant to the headmaster and teaches Humanities, she said this about her career at Newman: "There has never been a single day that I have not been thrilled to be here."

*"We did* Threepenny Opera *and* Oklahoma, *and I remember thinking at the time that this didn't seem like just some cruddy high school drama production. There were some very good voices, good acting and decent choreography. Lord knows we packed the house. And Mrs. Greenberg made it a lot of fun."*

Bryan Chaffe '83 agreed: "The productions were professional quality," he said. "Kitty Greenberg really tried to take me under her wing — I was a rebel without a cause in high school."

In 1976, Mr. Cunningham announced his resignation. In an interview with the *Greenie,* board Chairman Frank Friedler Jr. alluded to differences the headmaster had with the trustees. And Mr. Cunningham admitted "his total loss of contact with the student body." In his letter of resignation, he said, "I am convinced that my work at Newman has reached a plateau, and the time has come for me to move on."

Theodore Cotonio III, the Upper School Principal, was appointed acting Headmaster for the 1976–77 school year. He immediately announced his plans to apply for the permanent position.

# NEWMAN SCHOOL DAYS

*BY MICHAEL LEWIS '78*

*In New Orleans, Michael Lewis is known as the son of Newman alumni Tom and Diana Monroe Lewis, both class of 1955. Around the country, he is known as a best-selling author, most recently of* Moneyball. *After Newman, Michael earned an undergraduate degree in art history from Princeton and a master's degree in economics from the London School of Economics. He spent three years working on Wall Street before he left to become a writer. He is the author of* Liar's Poker *and* The New New Thing; *he has made television documentaries for the BBC; he has been an editor and a writer at several major magazines, and is currently a contributing writer to* The New York Times Magazine *and a columnist for* Bloomberg News. *He lives in Berkeley, California, with his wife, Tabitha Soren, a photographer and television journalist, and his two daughters, Quinn and Dixie.*

NOT UNTIL MY FRESHMAN YEAR in college did it occur to me that it was in any way unusual for an Episcopalian child to spend his first thirteen school years in a manual training school for Jewish orphans. Outside of New Orleans there weren't many WASPs who grew up spinning dreidels, lighting Menorahs and celebrating Rosh Hashanah. But maybe the most original aspect of the goy's experience of the Isidore Newman School was his experience of anti-Semitism. By "experience" I don't mean he witnessed the thing firsthand; I mean he was actually on the receiving end of it. When my Newman baseball team walked into some alien ballpark the fans and even the players from the other team would occasionally holler at us "Jewman! Jewman! Jewman!" I never understood why it counted as an insult to be identified as Jewish (one of Newman's many gifts to me), but that was beside the point. Their slurs were intended as insults, and so were, by definition, insulting. They left me strangely predisposed to stand and fight on behalf of my fellow Jews. Even stranger, I feel that way to this day.

But it would be wrong to dwell here on the religious flavor of the Newman experience, for it really was very faint. Newman was, above all, a vehicle for raising children's self-expectations. I realize this more in retrospect than I did at the time because at the time, Newman was all I knew. But looking back on it, I am struck by how my experience was defined by the sense that there was some high jumping bar out there that I was failing conspicuously to leap over. I recall being hauled before a Lower School principal (Miss Devlin) to explain why no one could read my handwriting. Then again, the next day, to explain to her why I thought it was so funny that in the first five minutes of third grade Phinizy Percy (nephew of the late novelist, Walker) had hit our teacher in the neck with a spitball. I recall standing before a Middle School principal (Mr. Schick) who demanded to know why the book report I had handed in of *Johnny Tremain* was an exact replica of that book's dust jacket copy;

and when I explained that I couldn't see how any book could be described any better by me than by its publisher, hearing him say that I should be expelled. I recall, a year later, somehow stumbling across a printout of the IQ's of some of my Middle School classmates. God knows how this happened, but it did. And I remember seeing that mine was the smallest number on the page and thinking, "Oh Christ, I'm a moron!" I remember having similar sensations upon receiving my grades, PSAT scores, SAT scores, and also in watching other people, not me, accept the seemingly endless awards for good character and academic achievement.

The interesting thing about all this temporary failure is that it never added up to the permanent kind. Newman, thank goodness, turned a blind eye to the less forgiving passages of the Talmud; indeed, at some point in its history, the school had assimilated one article of early Christian doctrine, a belief in the redemption of souls. It took the better part of eleven years for the institution to understand that mine was a soul in need of saving, but finally it did. And the place went to work on me, in a way that only a first-rate school can do. I recall many inspirational meetings in the headmaster's office in which I listened to the great man (Teddy Cotonio, who had personally interceded to spare me from Mr. Schick's death sentence) explain that, despite the overwhelming evidence to the contrary, I had big things in store for me in life. I recall genuine intellectual passion, kindled by a math teacher (Sheila Collins) and a historian named Arthur White, who used a course on the History of Western Religion to light fires inside the soggy minds of sixteen year olds. And I recall something like a moral and spiritual re-education program run on the baseball field by Billy Fitzgerald. Anyone who ever played anything for Fitz has a story to tell. I have many, and I'm saving them for my memoir which, thanks to the literary fine-tuning done by Newman school, I may actually think up myself, and write legibly.

The people who taught and coached at Newman changed me from a lazy boy who won no prizes because he failed to try, into an enthusiastic boy who won no prizes because he was not, in fact, terribly gifted. I'm pretty sure I should be grateful for it, but above all I am *impressed*. You see, I know the size of the job they had on their hands. The miracle they accomplished was no less than if they had redirected the Mississippi River twenty miles from its mouth, or taken Hamlet, re-written the last act, and made it into a side-splitting comedy. However I might have turned out without their help, I would have been a less useful citizen than I am now. And that's saying something.

*Teddy Cotonio, English teacher, head of the Upper School and headmaster, 1968 to 1986.*

# CHAPTER NINE

# TCIII

*I'm probably the school's biggest admirer. Newman's greatest strength is Newman.*

Theodore Cotonio III,
*Newman headmaster, 1976–1986.*

ein | McLeod

*LEFT: Varsity Quiz Bowl, 1979–80.*

HE HAS BEEN DESCRIBED as larger than life, as the embodiment of Newman. He inspired passionate opinions, both positive and negative, but no one can deny the profound impact Teddy Cotonio had on the school in the seventies and eighties. He left an indelible mark on Newman, changing both the physical plant and the very character of the school.

Teddy Cotonio was born in 1933 in New Orleans, where he grew up on Palmer Avenue and attended public and parochial schools. He received his B.A. in English and history and a law degree from Tulane, but he practiced law for only two years before he decided what he really wanted was to be a teacher. He taught at Jesuit and Rummel Catholic High School, eventually becoming chairman of Rummel's English department. He was lured away in 1968 by Louis Lemle, then chairman of Newman's board. The Lemles took Mr. Cotonio and his wife, Asta, to lunch at Manale's and convinced him to take a pay cut to teach English at Newman.

He was instantly liked by his new students. David Sylvester '74 said he made Russian literature come alive: "I remember riding home on the bus and reading Dostoyevsky and thinking, 'Man, is this amazing.'" The 1971 *Absinthe* was dedicated to him; editors said he was "unusually accessible for both general discussion and serious counsel. He has opened his house and his classroom to each of us. He has stood up for us when others have been critical." Lou Good '71 remembers stopping by the Cotonio residence on a regular basis. "We used to go over there all the time. You could just sit and talk to him. And we loved Asta, his wife." Mrs. Cotonio said students were drawn to her husband's charisma and intelligence: "He was so communicative and so interested. No one could ever make Teddy out to be a saint. But it was his humanness and his ability to understand a person that was so special."

In 1972, when Mrs. Shultz decided to concentrate solely on guidance counseling, Mr. Cotonio was appointed to take her place as principal of the Upper School. An editorial in the *Greenie* revealed some students' unhappiness with the choice. Mr. Cotonio was perceived as conservative, and therefore hostile to "liberals" and "long hairs." The editorial said Mr. Cotonio picked favorites, and they usually were athletes. Shortly after the editorial ran, the faculty advisor to the student paper was fired. It was rumored he was terminated because he allowed the editorial to run, and the school was divided for a time over the issue. But the furor died down and four years later, when Mr. Cunningham resigned, Mr. Cotonio took his place as headmaster. When his permanent appointment was announced, many students celebrated with a parade.

Meanwhile, perhaps in the hopes of someday becoming headmaster, the young Mr. Cotonio traveled to Hattiesburg, Mississippi, after school for years to obtain a master's degree in school administration from the University of Southern Mississippi. He drove with Ralph Weddington and Coach Ed "Skeets" Tuohy, who were also working on advanced degrees. "We'd get out of school and get in the car and drive to Hattiesburg and go to school at night and drive home," Mr.

Weddington said. "We'd stop on the way and Teddy would get chili and a chocolate sundae — and eat them together! One bite of one, one of the other. He had a stomach of steel."

Kitty Greenberg said Mr. Cotonio often would eat pizza on his porch in the middle of the night, to avoid waking his wife. "He looked like a snowman," said Michael Lewis '78. "Even in New Orleans, he was always the biggest man in the room. And he was full of charm — a delightful character."

"He reminded me of the headmaster in the Archie comics," said Elizabeth Conway Philipson '83. "He was always walking the halls, with his glasses at the end of his nose, looking up." He liked to needlepoint things such as Christmas ornaments while he watched TV at night, Dave Prescott said. Mr. Cotonio once told Linda Gottesman Baum '67 that whenever he spoke in front of crowds, his toes would curl up tight in his shoes. Jay Lapeyre '71 said his English teacher could write equally well with his right and left hands, and he could add up huge columns of four-digit numbers in his head.

He was a wonderful dancer, and a charmer. "He was the kind of person who could talk to anybody at any level, about whatever you wanted to talk about," Mr. Prescott said. "If it was an Uptown woman who likes to salivate about Carnival, he would la-dee-da about who was going to be king or queen of this or that. And there was that personal touch, because he was the first headmaster who was a New Orleans native." Faculty parties at his home were festive. There was always one punch that was so strong, Mr. Prescott said, "You'd have to crawl home." The headmaster's house — a gift to the school, at 49 Versailles Boulevard, which remains the headmaster's home today — was immaculate and filled with family silver, always polished.

As a teacher, he was admired for his mind; as an administrator, he was revered for his attention to detail, and his way of making both grand and personal gestures. He was relentless in his mission to make the Palaestra and the football field a reality. He collected and framed more than 1,000 posters and hung them on the once-barren school walls. He had the idea to create a third floor out of the attic of the Valmont Building for science labs.

"He was clearly a unique person," Mrs. Greenberg said. "He was a Renaissance man, he knew everything. And he was bigger than life. You either basked in his glow or you were in the shadows. Faculty meetings were three hours of him talking. He was like the dictator of a small Latin American country. It was very entertaining, but it was sometimes hard to get things done."

Mr. Lapeyre spoke of his ability to light a fire in his students:

*Teddy Cotonio, Newman's headmaster, 1976–1986.*

*His greatest strength was that he could make kids believe they could achieve something they never would have imagined. I first met him when he was our home-room teacher. He had a big impact on our class. He just understood the insecurities of kids. He probably had a lot of them himself. I was quite content playing basket-ball and watching the world go by. But he was relentless. He would say you could do well in school and you could try out for a drama production. He'd do this with dozens of kids, and he would track them consistently. He simply wouldn't allow you to slip through a crack.*

Many who knew Mr. Cotonio speak of his ability to push and congratulate, often in the same breath. "He had a huge influence on me," Mr. Sylvester said. "He was always pushing me. He was always saying, 'You're a smart kid and you will go places.' He would constantly tell me that, making sure I saw my potential."

In an interview with *New Orleans CityBusiness* in 1982, Mr. Cotonio said:

*The school can function not just as an academic base for children during childhood, adolescence and early adulthood, but as a place where you develop the psychological and emotional aspects of the person — how they feel about themselves. It's very important to make children feel good about themselves, not just teach them skills. The family has the primary responsibility for this, but schools should be a partner. That's not all new, but I've emphasized it more than before.*

153

Gerald Williams '81 called his headmaster a mentor.

*I remember him pulling me into his office and instilling the confidence in me that I could be mayor of New Orleans or whatever I wanted to be. He was a dynamic leader, and he had an agenda to put Newman on the map — athletically, academically, and as a place that had a great impact on New Orleans. I think he achieved that goal. Some say he wanted to create an Uptown, elitist atmosphere, but I never experienced that.*

Mr. Cotonio was a sports fanatic, going to as many games as he could, keeping score in his own unique way and promoting girls' athletics as much as boys'. As well as he knew every student, he also knew what sport each one played. But faculty and alumni said the arts also flourished under his leadership. Bryan Batt '81, who was active in drama and not at all athletic, said he had a close relationship with Mr. Cotonio. "He was very supportive and very kind," he said. Mrs. Cotonio said her husband "loved everything Newman did. He loved the plays, the music, the debating."

Finally, he was extremely competitive. He wanted Newman to stand out in the community and beyond. He wanted his students to take pride in their school. "He really wanted this school to be the best in the city," said Sheila Collins, who has taught math at Newman since 1972 and is now the department chair. Under his watch, Newman was recognized as one of 281 exemplary schools in the United States by the U.S. Secretary of Education. It was one of only seventeen private, non-sectarian schools chosen. Mr. Cotonio traveled to Washington for the award ceremony at the White House.

His competitiveness trickled down to the students, in positive and negative ways. "He created Newman's confidence in Newman," said Tim Williamson '83. "He made us think we were better than everybody else, for better or for worse." While the students excelled more than ever, and in more ways than ever, they had a reputation for being "viciously competitive, academically and socially," said Michael Lewis. "We were known as the mean school." Monte Lemann '79 said, "A lot of people looking back would regard Newman as a tough place." Some students recall with pain that if you didn't measure up to the current standard of what was cool, you were mocked, or worse — you became invisible.

Mr. Cotonio may have had the starring role in his day, but there were some important supporting cast members. Here is a look at just a few of the memorable teachers from the era.

Warreene Dart was the Mary Poppins of Newman — full of surprises, full of tricks to capture young imaginations and full of joy. She taught second grade for fifteen years, and she is pretty sure that's the best grade at Newman. "They're just getting all their basic reading skills and math skills," she said. "Once they have that, they can do anything. We did all sorts of wild things."

Her children toured oil wells and rode in hot air balloons. They strolled the French Quarter, flew kites and had a Pow-Wow in Danneel Park. She started lasting traditions, such as the annual trip to Ponchatoula to pick strawberries, Christmas Around the World and the live chess tournament, where children posed as game pieces. Children created puppets of famous people in history and made their parents guess who they were. "I remember Bryan Batt doing Michelangelo and making his puppet say, 'Oh! My back is so stiff from painting this ceiling all day!'" she said.

*A group of Newman children from the early 1960s.*

"She encouraged me theatrically," Mr. Batt said. "She would leave fifteen minutes free on Tuesdays and I would write a play or someone else would, and we'd put it on." Also, Mrs. Dart would pull a name out of a hat and then turn on a tape recorder, said Sabrina Forman Pilant '88, and everyone in the class would say something about that person. "I remember someone saying, 'She's fun to play house with,'" she said.

Warreene Tutt Dart was a native of New Orleans educated in the local Catholic schools. At the end of World War II, she joined the Red Cross and was stationed in Europe. "We crossed over on the Queen Mary with men on their way to try war criminals in Nuremberg," she said. When she returned, she was a medical secretary until she married and began to have children. In 1967, after teaching kindergarten at Holy Name for eight years, she spoke with Miss Devlin about an opening in the second grade at Newman. She was hired and remained there until her retirement in 1982.

"The kids were so wonderful," she said. "Their minds were like little sponges." Her admiration did not end when students left her class. "I do book signings and she shows up," said Mr. Lewis, a bestselling author whose works include *Liar's Poker* and *Moneyball*. "She made me sign, 'To Mrs. Dart, You didn't teach me any of the words on pages . . .' and she named the pages where there were four-letter words."

Fifth-grade teacher Helene Plotkin continued in that nurturing tradition. "She made learning interesting and gave me so much encouragement," said Merritt Lane '79. Keith Miller '79, agreed: "She was my favorite. She probably got the most out of

*Warreene Dart, second-grade teacher from 1967 to 1982.*

me. And she got my parents involved and engaged. She was the kind of person who would say, 'You don't think you can do it but you can.'"

History teacher Arthur White left a lasting impression on Mr. Lewis. "He taught a history of Western Religion course that was just electric for me," he said.

"He was pretty quirky," said Bryan Chaffe '83. "He filled the class with stories of the sexual proclivities of the popes and kings of Medieval Europe. Historical figures became real people you could relate to, because they had the same kinds of strange inclinations as the people in today's world. And he adopted Jimmy Stewart's rabbit, 'Harvey,' as a foil." Other students remember Harvey. "He'd always ask, 'Where is Harvey sitting? With the girls of course!'" said Ashley Keller Nelson '83. "He was just delightful."

CLOCKWISE FROM TOP LEFT: *Arthur White, history teacher from 1979 to 1987. Sheila Collins, who came to Newman as a math teacher in 1972 and is today chairman of the department. She also holds the Joseph C. Morris teaching chair. Pierson Marshall, a science teacher who began in 1972. Elizabeth Francis, English teacher from 1974 to 1991. Kate Barron, who came to Newman as an English teacher in 1977 and is today head of the Humanities program.*

Kate Barron began teaching English in 1977 and today is head of the Humanities program. "She was easy-going," Mrs. Nelson said. Mrs. Philipson remembers her energy in class. "She really made you appreciate what you were reading," she said. Robert Johnston '86 said Mrs. Barron used to assign his class five pages a week in a journal, in addition to the usual writing assignments. "More than anything else I learned, I think about that; that's how I learned how to write," he said. "She was teaching us how to boil down our thoughts and how to organize everything." Today, Mrs. Barron has students write in a journal daily, at the beginning of class. "My hope is that they create a record of their year, but many write stories or poems as they please," she said. Her goal is to teach writing through both traditional and non-traditional tasks. She assigns students to write chapters in the style of authors they are studying, for example.

Elizabeth Francis was the terrifying English teacher of the day, called "a chip off the old Mrs. Grout block" by Mr. MacKenzie. "She was exacting and demanded excellence," Mr. Lewis said. Tim Williamson, who said he would often get an F on a paper because of a misplaced comma, appreciates Dr. Francis today. "She was into the details of excellence, and that was so much of what Newman was about," he said. Gerald Williams agreed: "She was tremendous. She had high standards and she didn't compromise. I still remember having to recite the prelude to *Beowulf* and I can still recite it to this day. I struggled with Cs with her, but when I got to college, I made As in English."

Sheila Collins inspired similar terror and respect — and continues to do so to this day. She began her career at Newman in 1972 teaching geometry and algebra. A graduate of Benjamin Franklin High School, Newcomb and Tulane, where she earned a Ph. D., Dr. Collins admits she is a tough teacher, but she says it is because she is determined that everyone in her classes excel. "I want to really teach them some math that they can use in their lives and not be afraid of," she said. "I don't want kids to get to college and say, 'I don't want to major in that because I'd have to take some math.'"

"She was very strict in class but outside of class she was a really nice person," said Lisa Lupin '86. "And she bent over backwards to help you learn the math."

She may seem deadly serious at first, but Dr. Collins is not without her fun side. "Want to see my cage?" she asked a visitor recently, as though this were a normal question for a math teacher to ask. She pulled from her cabinet a bird cage, inside of which was perched a "torture victim." She then hauled out a box of creatures — small rubber animals, monsters and the like. In class, when someone gave a wrong answer, she used to take a creature and, using it to symbolize the student, place it inside the cage with the victim on the perch, which was supposed to be her — the "tortured teacher."

"She had these things she did that made you think she was just a little bit crazy and unpredictable," said Michael "Corky" Stone '91. "Somebody would be giving an answer that was completely incorrect, or someone would be really misbehaving, and she would open her desk drawer and pull out one of these figurines and place it on her desk, and open up the other drawer and pull out a hammer and start smashing the figurine. Another time she very deliberately threw a figurine out the window. It was funny."

Her explanation: "Math can be dry."

After class, everyone talked about her and told their parents, Mr. Stone said. "It was a thing that made you remember her and made you think about her. I'm about to start teaching myself, and I think a lot about her. She was so scary but you wanted to do well in her class."

Pierson Marshall, a science teacher from central Louisiana, also began his Newman career in 1972, and still teaches today. In 1972, chemistry and physics were electives, and he was the only teacher for both subjects. "He made chemistry fun," Mr. Williams said. That may be an understatement, according to others. "He'd explode things in the back of the room," Mrs. Nelson said. "While he was lecturing, he would throw exploding rocks on the floor and if you could walk across them without setting one off, you'd get an A — or so he said. I did it, but I didn't get an A."

Mr. Marshall laughs about his students' oft-heard plea: "Blow something up Mr. Marshall." Science is difficult and it's tough to maintain interest, he said. "One thing about science is we have a lot of tricks. We have a whole cosmos full of tricks. I try to come up with ways of setting something on fire, or when they go to sleep in class have something explode. That way they look forward to coming back to class."

"He was wild," said Elizabeth Conway Philipson. "It seemed like he had the periodic table written on his glasses, because whenever he wanted to recall an element, he'd look up like he was looking at them." By his own example, Mr. Marshall has always shown his students how science is applicable to everyday life. Science led him to become an expert at restoring houses — namely his own. He even designed an irrigation system and an alarm system for his renovated double. Science led him to an interest in photography; he was chosen to study with Ansel Adams one summer in Yosemite National Park. He taught photography at Newman, and created a class in photojournalism. And for years he has been a consultant to jewelry designer Mignon Faget.

Ken MacKenzie was still inspiring fear and respect in the eighties. "Something about him made you want to do well and made you want to learn," said Michael Stone. "His course as much as anything prepared me for college."

And Dave Prescott, who had become the librarian, continued to be a student favorite. He took over for Miss Wadsworth in 1976. The library then had 27,000 books; today, it has 50,000 in the main library and another 20,000 in the Lower School library. "He would leave the library open a couple of nights a week for studying," said Mrs. Philipson. "He'd always say, 'You're vocalizing!'"

With World War II decades in the past, Frank Cernicek, now an old man, seemed even more exotic to this new generation. "He used to call me 'Battnik,'" said Bryan Batt. "We would beg to hear stories of his years in Nazi-occupied Europe. He would say that he was going to tell us, but later. He'd say 'Wait, it is coming.'"

"It was a rite of passage to make it through eighth grade geography," said Mrs. Nelson. "You'd memorize the world in twenty-four to forty-eight hours and then you forgot it. And every day, he pinched my cheek. So on the last day of class, I pinched him back." She also remembers people placing their pens on the edges of their desks so that when Mr. Cernicek would pace, as he did continuously, the pens would mark his pants. By the end of a semester, his pants were stained with a rainbow of ink.

In the late seventies, Jimmy Carter was in the White House, Edwin Edwards was in his second of four terms as governor, and Ernest Morial had just been elected the first black mayor of New Orleans. The city was enjoying a building boom and economic prosperity thanks to the rise in oil prices. A few years into Mr. Cotonio's tenure, Newman celebrated its seventy-fifth anniversary with a gala at the Fairmont Hotel, new landscaping, the restoration of the front doors to their original look, and a fundraising drive to pay for Newman's own building boom. In 1979, there were eleven buildings on campus, 1,000 students, and 100 faculty and staff. The annual fund was at more than $140,000, and the capital fund had raised more than $3 million toward a goal of $5 million. Gifts included the first endowed teaching chairs: the Joseph C. Morris Chair in physics and math and the William B. Wisdom Chair in English. They went to math teacher Sheila Collins and English teacher David Waters. Dr. Collins has a portrait of Dr. Morris in her classroom; she tells her students it is "Captain Calculus." Also that year, the faculty and staff pledged $50,000 for scholarships.

The school embarked on an ambitious plan to enlarge the endowment, then at $365,000. The school also planned to build a new physical education facility, to buy two blocks of Dufossat Street for a regulation football field, and to turn the girls' gym into a fine arts center. In 1980, construction began on the gym, slated to cost $3.2 million. The 50,000-square-foot Palaestra was to be a state-of-the-art facility complete with an arena for volleyball and basketball, a girls' gym, and a swimming pool, something administrators had been promising students since 1919. It opened in 1981, dramatically changing not only athletics but the feel of the campus. A year later, a patio was constructed outside the Palaestra, giving students a new place to congregate. That same year, the old girls' gym was converted into the Charles Keller III Memorial Center for Fine Arts. It was named for a Newman alumnus, parent and board member.

As the administration worked on these dramatic changes to the campus, students were dancing to Bruce Springsteen and Led Zeppelin and getting acquainted with disco. In the seven-

*Cheerleaders, 1984.*

160

*LEFT: Newman teachers at the Y.O. Ranch outdoor awareness program in Texas. RIGHT: A student rappels at Y.O. Ranch.*

ties, the junior-senior prom night began with a multi-course meal at Commander's Palace, followed by dancing at the New Orleans Lawn Tennis Club and a breakfast at someone's home. Certain traditions were set in stone by the seventies: freshmen always had a cookie sale, sophomores hosted the bazaar, and juniors washed cars. Homecoming was as important as ever, but it was evolving. In 1979, a new election procedure was put in place: all senior girls were on a ballot and all seniors could vote for the court. The Upper School then voted for the queen. By the early eighties, boys were elected to the court as well.

The Washington trip was still a tradition, and starting in 1978, eighth-graders went to the Y.O. Ranch in Texas for an outdoor awareness program. "It was the first time I was ever stretched both physically and emotionally," Mrs. Pilant said.

Social life revolved around the Friday night football game and the open houses afterward, said Mrs. Philipson. "We used to rent buses to go to away games. It was really fun. Even if they lost, we'd go back to the gym locker rooms and clap for them. Sometimes there were even tears in the players' eyes." By the early 1980s, the girls weren't just cheering: they were partici-

161

pating in varsity volleyball, cross country, basketball, soccer, track, tennis and swimming.

Newman students who lived near school still went home for lunch, as they had been doing for generations. "My mother would expect anywhere from two to ten people home for lunch," Mrs. Nelson said.

"And this is what we'd eat," said Mrs. Philipson. "We'd take a brick of Cracker Barrel cheese and put it in the microwave and dip crackers in it. And watch *All My Children*." Mrs. Nelson said they were so addicted to the soap opera that they sometimes brought a radio to school if they could not go home for it. Robert Johnston said he and his friends went to Frankie & Johnny's for lunch. Or he would sneak into Country Day and eat lunch in their cafeteria. His motive? He was often dating a Country Day girl.

In 1981, tuition ranged from $2,475 to $3,500. Enrollment in the early eighties was around 1,100. Ronald Reagan became president, and the news of the day was the Cold War and the possibility of a nuclear attack on the United States. In December, 1983, the administration sent a note home to parents advising them to supervise their children if they watched *The Day After*, a television movie about a nuclear attack on the United States. The local economy suffered as oil prices fell and the state's energy industry floundered. In 1984, New Orleans hosted a world's fair, but attendance and revenue were a huge disappointment. New Wave music, Miss Pacman, hackey sack and the preppie look were in. Most Newman students could be recognized by their "uniform," the male version of which was sketched and explained in the *Greenie*. It included a cashmere scarf, Lee corduroy jeans or khakis, "held up by a (school enforced) belt, which usually has whales or ducks head to tail," and Wallabees shoes. In some ways, socializing had not changed

at all in several generations. Newman boys were still shooting pool at Robert's, a bar off of Claiborne Avenue. And a favorite hangout for the class of 1983 was the basement of Pete Moss's grandmother's home near City Park — the very same basement where Mr. Moss's mother, Andrée Keil Moss '55, and her Newman classmates used to gather. Student pranks had a familiar look, at least to those who know their Newman history. A yellow Volkswagen bug found its way to the senior patio, said Lisa Lupin. "And then there were those chickens on the patio. They weren't happy about that."

Continuing an old tradition, Newman excelled in debating in the late seventies and eighties. In 1977–78, Newman students won more than twenty-five trophies in nineteen tournaments nationwide. The school was asked to represent Louisiana in a national tournament in Philadelphia in 1978. Newman also enjoyed a long run of victories in the city-wide Prep Quiz Bowl.

In 1981, four new classes were added to the curriculum — accounting, anthropology, A.P. literature and ecology. Robert Johnston remembers a class in film history in the eighties. In 1984, Chinese was offered, thanks to a grant from the Geraldine R. Dodge Foundation. Today, Newman remains the only school in Louisiana to teach four years of Chinese. In 1985, MACOS — Man, a course of study — was introduced to the fifth grade by Peter Massony, again thanks to a grant, this time from the Ford Foundation and the National Science Foundation. MACOS taught the differences between man and other species by observing baboon videos, then observing younger children on the playground, and finally by having the students act out a baboon society. They also recorded general observations from the world around them in journals.

In 1985, a long-range planning committee issued a report called Newman 2000. The committee saw a need to strengthen

*Members of the class of 1987.*

LEFT: *Greenies at play on Michael Lupin Field.* INSET: *A drawing of Lupin Field.* ABOVE: *Class of 1988 forming an 88 at the last moment of their last day of school.*

language instruction; to spend more time developing each individual student; to raise the endowment to $20 million by 2000; to work harder to reflect in the student population the changing demographics of New Orleans; to make the entire campus handicap accessible; to decide what to do about the outdated Stern Building; to make more library space, and to find a place for a baseball/softball diamond.

Also in 1985, Michael Lupin Field was dedicated to the memory of a seventeen-year-old who died of cancer in 1972.

He did not attend Newman but many other Lupins did. Mayor Morial spoke at the dedication. "The field and the Palaestra were a huge thrill," said Robert Johnston. "Student life became a lot more focused on campus."

At the center of all of this expansion and change was Teddy Cotonio, leading the way, pulling the strings, pushing and congratulating. Eventually, Mrs. Greenberg said, "He thought he *was* the school."

And for many people, he was.

# BEAUTIFUL MINDS

*BY SARAH LABOUISSE EVANS '84*

*Sarah Labouisse Evans was not a member of the debate team at Newman. She was a volleyball, soccer and tennis team member, as well as a glutton for punishment who, after surviving the Sophomore Bazaar, decided that it would also be fun to edit the* Absinthe *her senior year. She went on to receive a B.A. in History from Princeton University in 1988 and an M.A. in American History from Stanford University in 1991. She has worked (and still does, periodically) as a researcher and writer for the National Geographic Society and Time-Life Books, and is currently employed at the Baltimore Zoo as an exhibit writer. She lives in Baltimore with her husband and former Newman classmate, Hugh Evans '84, and their three children.*

THERE CAN BE NO DOUBT, in the mind of anyone who was paying attention, that the most successful competitive team at Newman while I was there was the debate team. Those of us who sat through weekly Upper School assemblies knew this intuitively, if not definitively, based on the reports given by team captains. Every Monday morning of my senior year, the debate team co-captains would lug some enormous trophy to the front of the auditorium and chronicle their most recent wins. One had the air of a very young college professor, in button-down plaid shirt and sweater vest with hands stuffed in the pockets of his corduroy jeans. The other stood slightly hunched in a khaki trench coat, gazing out at the crowd, always with the discernible hint of a cat-who-stole-the-canary grin on his face. These two would tell where the team had traveled over the weekend — to Houston, to Duke University, to Cambridge, England perhaps — and then acknowledge each teammate who had placed first, second or third in one or another forensics category.

Week by week, those of us in the audience listening came to appreciate that we were in the presence of competitive greatness. It didn't matter that we were vague on the definition of "extemporaneous" and had no clue what was meant by "Lincoln-Douglas Debate." We could remain stupefied by the categories and still wonder, on the off week, how it was possible that so-and-so had failed to place or that our previously indomitable Duo Interpretation team had managed to come up short.

I knew to be impressed by the debate team not only because of their many far-flung victories but also because of the intellectual caliber of those team members who were also my classmates.

Take the trench coat-clad co-captain, for example. He had one of the sharpest minds I've ever encountered, then or since. Pick your subject. No concept seemed to confound him, no measure of literary genius escaped his powers of interpretation, no fact was too obscure for his recall.

And yet, in my class of 101, he had peers. He had rivals. He was not the only one who could actually visualize trigonometric principles or offer a convincing, impromptu explanation of why pigeons strut. He was not the one quietly writing nationally-acclaimed poetry even before we graduated, or the one dancing with a professional ballet company, or the one whose humor and wit were just so brilliantly odd that they seemed destined one day to inspire a syndicated cartoon.

Even the quality of my peers' subterfuge was impressive. The school newspaper's "Greenie Gourmets" come to mind. Doesn't it take a certain amount of creative genius to vividly describe the ambience of a particular restaurant or the sensation of crème caramel melting on the tongue if, in fact, you've never had crème caramel and you never left your kitchen? If, in fact, your reviews were concocted solely from the imaginations and cookbooks at hand? "Veritable boatloads of salad" no less.

To put it simply, I met some of the smartest, funniest, and most entertaining people of my life in high school. Several of them remain my closest friends. Maybe this makes you question the quality of the company I've kept since; you might wonder whether it's been nothing but a downhill slide since I left Newman. I wouldn't say so. I would just say that I got very lucky to have had peers who made the days interesting and to have made friends that I'll keep for life. For this I am still thankful, because my life has been better for it.

ABOVE: *Two members of Newman's successful forensics team.*
FOLLOWING SPREAD: *Class of 1983.*

*Football players from an era when the school was still Isidore Newman Manual Training School.*

# CHAPTER TEN

# In the Game: Athletics at Newman

—◦◦◦—

*Play hard, play smart, and play together.*

COACH BILLY FITZGERALD

*LEFT TO RIGHT: Athletics at Newman: shown here are basketball, volleyball, football and cross country.*

THE EARLY HISTORY of Newman athletics is not rich with stories of victory — although for a small school, the Greenies had their fair share of wins. It is the story of heroes, on the field and on the sidelines: the young coach who became the father of prep football in New Orleans, the one-armed football player from the 1930s and the Czech tennis instructor who once played with kings. In more recent years, Newman has been fortunate to have both heroes and state championships, all the while maintaining uncompromising academic standards.

"The sports program is not fascinating because of all the championships we've won," said former board Chairman Darryl Berger '65. "It's fascinating that a school with the most rigorous academic requirements could also produce excellent teams. That is unusual. It's a remarkable testament to the overall quality of the school, and the diverse capacity to succeed there."

Football and basketball were the first sports played at Isidore Newman Manual Training School. Football began in 1907, not many years after the game was introduced to New Orleans youth. Claude "Monk" Simons Sr., a legend in New Orleans football, coached the boys from 1911 through 1917. After he left Manual, he helped form the city's first prep school athletic league, and later was a trainer for

*LEFT: Claude "Monk" Simons Sr., Manual's coach from 1911 to 1917, photo from* The Golden Game, When Prep Football was King in New Orleans. *Photo by Leon M. Trice. RIGHT: Maurice Garb, Newman student who played football in the 1930s, despite having only one arm. Drawing from* The Golden Game, When Prep Football was King in New Orleans.

Tulane's Green Wave football team. Those early teams, who wore green even then, held their own, often vying for, but never winning, the city championship.

The Greenies rose to some prominence in the late twenties and early thirties, thanks to Coach Jack Orsley and some outstanding athletes. In 1929, the Greenies defeated rival Rugby 40-0, and in 1930, they won their first Class B league championship. Those winning teams had two stars — Bernard "Barney" Mintz and Claude "Little Monk" Simons Jr. They both went on to play for Tulane and win top honors in the first Sugar Bowl game. Monk Simons Jr. was Tulane's football coach during World War II.

The 1933 team finished third in the league under a new coach, but that wasn't the most remarkable thing about the Greenies that year. Maurice Garb, who lived at the Jewish Children's Home, was a guard and a linebacker, despite having only one arm. He lost his arm under an ice cream wagon in his home town in Texas. According to an account in *The Golden Game,* a book about prep football in New Orleans, his speed made up for his disability. In the book, teammate Ira Harkey '35, the Greenie quarterback who would go on to become a Pulitzer Prize-winning journalist, called him "exceptional. He kept moving his feet on offense . . . On defense, he had a way of grabbing (a ball-carrier) with one arm, then wrapping himself around the guy with his legs and letting his weight take the runner down." Newspapers from as far away as Oregon ran stories about Mr. Garb, who also played basketball and baseball.

In 1939, Newman joined the newly-formed Riverside League. The Greenies won the league football championships of 1943, 1948 and 1960. The victories of the forties were thanks to Coach Ralph "Smiley" Harris, who came to Newman after decades at rival New Orleans Academy. In 1948, the Greenies made it all the way to the state playoffs for the first time in Newman football history.

*ABOVE: 1948 Riverside Champions. RIGHT: Members of the Class of 1949 at their fiftieth reunion with the above photograph and trophy.*

*Coach Jack Orsley, a Newman coach in the 1920s and 1930s, pictured here with a Greenie baseball team from the 1920s.*

Newman always fared well in basketball. Ralph Harris was the coach of both basketball and football; Pat Samuels '42 remembers playing for him. "We played Rugby Academy, New Orleans Academy, Slidell and Westwego," he said. "We all shot underhand with two hands. In those days, you were a show off if you shot with one hand." In 1955, the Greenies won their first state basketball championship in class A. It was thanks to a "thrilling" game against La Salle High of Olla, where Newman won 49-48 thanks to a jump shot in the final seconds by Conrad Collins '56 according to the *Greenie*.

Newman won many tennis championships beginning in the forties, thanks in large part to the most intriguing athletic figure in Newman history — Francis Soyka. Under Mr. Soyka, Newman's tennis teacher and coach for decades beginning in 1940, the Newman tennis team won the Riverside crown every year from 1940 to 1955. "He taught us great form," said Andrée Keil Moss '55. "There are people today you can see playing and you can tell he taught them forehand and backhand. I lettered in tennis at Tulane and I attribute that to Mr. Soyka's teaching."

Francis Soyka was born in 1892 in Prague to a wealthy family of champagne makers. He was a gifted tennis player who faced the likes of King Gustav of Sweden and frequented the courts of the great resorts and spas of Europe. He won hundreds of trophies and awards, and was captain of the Czech Davis Cup team. In World War I, he served in the cavalry for the Austro-Hungarian Empire, and was decorated by Emperor Franz Joseph for his service. He always kept a picture of the emperor in his New Orleans home. When the Germans occupied Sudetenland in 1939, Francis Soyka was playing tennis abroad, and decided to go to the United States rather than return home. He brought little besides his tennis racket. The forty-eight-year-old tennis star, a son of wealth and privilege,

was suddenly penniless and without any means to support himself. He landed a summer job as a tennis instructor at Camp Androscoggin in Maine. A camper's parents then invited him to New Orleans to teach private lessons at Newman, promising that the mild weather meant he could play year round.

With his floppy white hat, his tennis whites, his harmlessly flirtatious and courtly manner and his trademark words — "Keep zee eye on zee ball" — he became a beloved Newman fixture. "This man of privilege and comfort, not a young man in 1940, utilized his experience and rebuilt a shattered life," Teddy Cotonio said in a eulogy on October 8, 1979. "He rebuilt his life and in doing so he retained his wit, charm and his courtly manner."

But even if you never played tennis and never walked by his courts, you would have known Mr. Soyka. His other talent was art; he drew countless images for Newman calendars, holiday cards and invitations. He wrote and illustrated a charming children's book about tennis. His art was so admired it would be auctioned off at Newman events.

He often would leave peppermints or cookies on people's desks, and he was also known for eating everyone's leftover lunches. "He saw so much waste, and always asked for our leftover lunches," Mrs. Moss said. "He was frugal." He lived modestly, in a small apartment where he liked to drink Dubonnet in the evenings, often raising his glass to Emperor Franz Joseph. He loved a good meal; the Rib Room was his favorite New Orleans restaurant. When he died, it was revealed he in fact had quite a lot of money. Unmarried and childless, he gave it all away; Newman received a house worth more than $200,000.

He adored Newman, and seemed always to be there. He told the *Pioneer* in 1948: "What do I think about Newman? The simple fact that I am even on rainy days at eight o'clock in

*Francis Soyka with the Newman tennis team, 1949.*

*An illustration by Newman tennis teacher, Francis Soyka.*

Ashley Keller Nelson '83. "I was on the tennis team and I would hear him in the back of my head, saying, 'Keep zee eye on zee ball.'"

*The New Orleans Times-Picayune* columnist Angus Lind '62 wrote this about Mr. Soyka in 1974: "Six days a week, Soyka still dons his trademarks — a floppy old white hat and sunglasses — and heads to Newman's tennis courts. There he sweeps the courts himself ('I told the janitor, "No thanks."') and puts in long hours working with the youngsters . . . Soyka loves teaching kids."

In 1974, the school celebrated his eighty-second birthday in grand style with a "Tennis Ball" and unveiled a portrait of him which now hangs in the arena. Phil Johnson of WWL-TV aired an editorial on him: "Who is Francis Soyka? He's the tennis coach at Newman School. But he is so much more. He is a magnificent man . . . athlete, artist, raconteur, with a wit and an accent quite European, yet a warmth and openness that is all American."

When he died October 6, 1979, there was a memorial for him at Newman. Someone hung a black wreath on the gate of the tennis courts. "Francis Soyka was a source of stability," the *Greenie* wrote. "No matter what was happening in the world, one could always count on seeing a little man in a floppy white hat, white sport shirt and slacks out on the court."

school shows how much I like the atmosphere and that I don't want to miss a single day with my young friends. Of course, especially the girls."

As the school grew and Mr. Soyka grew older, he stopped coaching tennis but continued to offer lessons until he died. "He didn't move very much but he returned everything," said

Another memorable character was Clarence "Chick" Henson, who coached and taught gym from 1935 until he died in 1971. The son of Principal Clarence Henson, and himself a 1929 Newman graduate, Chick Henson was everything his father was not: he was big and gregarious, goofy and colorful. His salty language and rapport with children made him a hero to his students; his too-short, too-tight gym shorts gave the

LEFT: *Clarence "Chick" Henson Jr., Newman gym teacher and coach from 1935 to 1971. He was the son of Principal Clarence C. Henson and was a 1929 graduate of Manual.* CENTER: *Anthony Reginelli, football coach and track coach, who began in 1961 and continues to coach part-time today.* RIGHT: *Ed "Skeets" Tuohy, Newman basketball and baseball coach, 1959 to 1975.*

administration fits.

"We just worshipped him," said Louis Fishman '59. "He drove a big, red Cadillac convertible with a white interior and he'd wear short satiny gym shorts. He was one of us. If we were playing baseball, he was the catcher. He was part of what made Newman great. I couldn't wait for gym class." Carol Hart '43 said, "For kids, Chick was quite a motivator, an inspiration. He had the presence and the bravado and every year he had a new convertible. He was fun." He was well known for losing his temper with the little kids, said David Stone '57. "My brother once told my mother he'd called his third-grade gym class 'a bunch of little Communist bastards'."

When he died, his junior varsity teams held the record for the greatest number of perfect, undefeated seasons in the state. "When he succumbed, many people, young and old, and a school, lost a lifelong friend," the *Greenie* said.

The rise in prominence of Newman athletics began in 1960 with the arrival of two coaches, Ed "Skeets" Tuohy and Anthony Reginelli. It was with Coach Tuohy, a tough-talking Irish-Catholic raised on the south side of Chicago, that the Newman basketball team really began to shine. "Everybody was scared to death of Skeets," Mr. Berger said. "When he was hot, he was really, really hot. That big Irish face of his would get red and you'd see the veins pop out on his head. But he was never abusive, even though he would get up in your face and say he was going to make a man out of you."

Growing up, Coach Tuohy played basketball at the Catholic schools in Chicago and came to New Orleans when he was recruited by Loyola. After college, he sold trucks for a year, and then he was hired to coach at Holy Cross. He came to Newman in 1959. And the championships began rolling in.

Newman won the 1961, '63 and '64 state basketball championships, thanks to a combination of great coaching and talented athletes. The year 1960–61 was a banner year for Newman: the football team won the Riverside league title after a perfect 8-0 season, the basketball team won state after a 32-0 season and Chick Henson's junior varsity basketball team won a championship. The senior *Pioneer* was dedicated to Coach Tuohy and Mr. Henson. The 1964 basketball team was nicknamed "Tuohy's Greenies" or "Snow White and the Four Dwarfs" with Bobby Lane, tall and blond, as Snow White. Mr. Lane '64 was named the most valuable player in the state in 1963, by which time he had scored well over 1000 points in his career.

Mr. Lane and many other alumni from this era say Coach Tuohy and Coach Reginelli had a profound influence on their lives. For Mr. Lind, who lost his father when he was a junior, they filled a void. "Newman's what kept me going, no doubt about it," said Mr. Lind, who managed the football and basketball teams. "And Skeets and Tony were the key. I would do things with them like a father and son would do. And, they changed the face of Newman athletics forever." Mr. Lind describes Coach Tuohy as "funny, funny. I would sit in the office with him and Tony just laughing." Mr. Lane called Coach Tuohy "a smart coach. He knew how to relate to the players. Most of us really got a lot out of the relationship."

David Sylvester '74 said Coach Tuohy could relate to him because both of them had grown up poor. "He would talk to me about what I was going through. He would tell me there are expectations in life, and here's how you look somebody in the eye when you shake their hand. He gave me really basic lessons that helped me."

In the early sixties, Coach Tuohy arranged a scrimmage with St. Augustine, an all-black school with a renowned basketball program. "We played them because the coach's attitude was that to get better you had to play good teams," Mr. Lane said.

*We couldn't play them in a real game because of segregation, but we scrimmaged them in our gym. The St. Aug players got there early on a Saturday morning and were waiting outside because the gym was locked. A panicked woman in the neighborhood called Coach Tuohy to report a bunch of "colored boys" on the steps of the gym. He said, "Oh? What color are they?" And he hung up.*

What was interesting, Mr. Lane said, was that even though the St. Augustine boys were better athletes, the Newman team was better coached. "My recollection is that we won, but that was less important than the fact that the scrimmage took place at all."

Everybody has a favorite Reginelli-ism — those funny, confusing little sayings of Tony Reginelli's that have become part of the Newman vernacular. There's his order to "line up alphabetically, by height." There's philosophy: "There are only two things that count: blocking, tackling and special teams." And the famous warning: "I don't want you guys going out there to the lake and throwing those beer cans in the river."

*Newman's 1960 football team, Riverside champions.*

*Photo by Leon M Trice.*

*Newman's basketball teams won a string of state championships in the early 1960s, including 1962–63.*

"I doubt any of us have as yet figured out what the difference is between a duck," said Merritt Lane '79.

"I kid around with the kids a lot. I make them think, 'Now what is he saying?'" said Coach Reginelli, explaining the meaning behind his words. "The more you make a student think, the less likely they are to take short cuts."

Coach Reginelli was young but "tough as nails" when he arrived to be assistant coach in 1961, Mr. Berger said. "He was tough physically but he was lovable all the time. He fussed, but with a loving touch." He would tell his players to walk off the field with their heads held high, even after a loss. "But what struck me as a kid is something I repeated to my four children, even in non-sports situations. After a win, he'd say, 'Let this go to your heart, not your head.'"

Tony Reginelli was born in Lake Village, Arkansas in 1934 and attended school in Shaw, Mississippi, just across the river. He was recruited by Tulane and played baseball there, making all-SEC. He graduated in 1957, but was hooked on New Orleans for good: "Once you got here, you got stuck in the mud, and the food just keeps you here. Then I married a New Orleans girl."

After college, he went into the service, and dreamed of playing professional baseball. But leagues were closing around the country, so when Holy Cross offered him a job working with Coach Tuohy, he took it. He then followed him to Newman. "He was a fun person to work with," said Coach Reginelli. "I didn't care about being head coach as long as I was around him." When he arrived at Newman, the school was, athletically, "a diamond in the rough." The school had no football field, so "every day was an away trip," he said. The team would pile themselves and all their equipment onto a bus headed for City Park. "It really wasn't as prominent athletically back then," he said. "It was known as an uppity, intellectual school. But I went to watch the kids play and I was impressed with the quality of the athletes."

When Coach Reginelli and Coach Tuohy arrived at Newman, the big football schools were Jesuit, Warren Easton and Holy Cross. Coach Tuohy was convinced Newman could compete with anybody, even in football. In the sixties, the Greenies began competing statewide and even made it to the state playoffs one year. "It was against University High, which was the lab school for LSU," Coach Reginelli said. "Skeets wanted to keep the game close, but we got behind, 14-0. Skeets came over and said, 'Tony! Dammit! I don't wanna lose this game by a big score!' We ended up winning 21-14. That was the first game we'd won in the playoffs. And it's gone on from there."

The football team never has won a state championship, but it has had plenty of winning seasons and has made it to the semifinals twice, in the seventies. One of those times, the Greenies lost to a school in Opelousas. The second time, they lost to St. Louis High School in Lake Charles. "It was so cold that day that the clock went out," Coach Reginelli recalled. "I hate to go back . . . we missed a touchdown pass in the last minute and a half. That was the most heartbreaking loss we ever had. The kid was really upset. We had a really long trip back. My son was on that team."

Like Coach Tuohy, Coach Reginelli is remembered by former players as a father figure whose influence changed lives, in all the right ways. Donald Ensenat '64, who is Chief of Protocol for the United States, said of his former coaches in a commencement speech: "They taught us that athletics was more than just winning sports games; it was about character and teamwork, the skills to succeed at the game of life."

GERRY DEFRAITES    MIKE PIPER    MAC McCALL    LEE TRICE

# LOUISIANA STATE CHAMPIONS
## MILE RELAY
## 1966

*Newman's track team won the state championship in the mile relay in 1966.*    *Photo by Leon M. Trice*

LEFT: *Billy Fitzgerald, basketball and baseball coach, and Middle School science teacher, 1973 to the present. He now coaches baseball only.*
CENTER: *Bobbie van der Giessen taught girls' physical education and oversaw the Girls Athletic Committee from 1960 until 1977.* RIGHT:
*Joanne Skertich came to Newman in 1974 to teach girls' intramural sports. She was instrumental in organizing varsity volleyball at
Newman. Today, she is an assistant admission director.*

"I try to teach every kid as if he's my own," Coach
Reginelli said.

> *You have to be fair, you have to be up front,
> because these kids are very intelligent. And my philos-
> ophy was we gotta make it fun. If it's miserable, they
> ain't gonna have fun. And I think a coach has to be a
> teacher. They are probably the best teachers, because they
> get closer to their students. But the correlation between
> athletics and academics goes hand in hand. When I
> first came here, athletics and academics were like oil
> and water. Teachers wouldn't even tell me hello. I
> wanted to bring Newman athletics up to the academic
> levels. Because if something good happens on the field,
> then a kid feels good about himself and it carries over to
> the classroom.*

Coach Reginelli used to argue with Mrs. Shultz that taking
athletics away from a struggling student was counter-produc-
tive. "I showed her that students actually do better when
they're involved in sports. They just need to learn to be better
organized with their time."

Coach Reginelli also turned track into a winning sport at
Newman. He organized the team in 1961 to give the boys
something to do in the spring. Newman excelled, placing
second in the district behind St. Martin's for almost a decade.

186

"We had a great relay team," he said. "We won state in the mile relay in the sixties."

In the sixties, Newman boys also participated in golf, swimming and tennis. The school joined the Louisiana High School Athletic Association and in 1968, Coach Tuohy was appointed athletic director and devoted himself to basketball while Coach Reginelli was named head football coach. The basketball team continued to win the district pennant almost annually.

By the late seventies, the Newman boys routinely were winning city tennis championships and district championships in soccer. They won their first cross-country state championship in 1978.

Baseball began in 1973, thanks to start-up funding from a parent. Coach Tuohy coached the new sport until he suffered a stroke in 1975. In 1982, he died of cancer at the age of forty-nine, right after the gym was renamed for him. Coleman E. Adler II '61 led the fundraising campaign for the name change; Coach Tuohy tried to attend the dedication ceremony but found he was too sick to get out of the car. He died two days later. "Coach Tuohy brought winning to Newman, and instilled a new pride in Newman athletics," reported the *Greenie* after his death.

After Coach Tuohy's stroke, a new coach took over baseball and basketball: Billy Fitzgerald. Coach Fitz had come to Newman in 1973 as an assistant basketball and baseball coach after playing minor league baseball. A New Orleans native, he was educated at Jesuit, where Teddy Cotonio was his teacher and mentor. When he went on to Tulane, Mr. Cotonio would attend almost all his baseball and basketball games. After school, he was drafted into the minor leagues by the Oakland A's, but when his first child, Edmond, was born, he and his wife decided

it was time to return home. Mr. Cotonio was there, waiting to offer him a job.

Coach Fitzgerald, who gave up basketball two years ago but remains the baseball coach, is tall and imposing and has a fierce temper. "The lesson he taught was that it's not supposed to be easy. It's supposed to be hard," Michael Lewis '78 said. "He scared the living hell out of every kid who played for him, and he made us feel like this was the most important thing on the planet." Even though Mr. Lewis hit puberty late and was not a good baseball player at first, his coach insisted his size was irrelevant. "He gave me a chance," he said. "He believed in me and he gave me opportunities to justify his faith in me." Mr. Lewis remembers a time when Coach Fitz put him in a game at a crucial moment; he helped win the game. "Fitz had decided I was someone who had guts," he said. "There was no higher compliment. I regard that moment as a turning point in my life. I started caring more about school; I was more focused, more determined." After graduation, Mr. Lewis went to Princeton, where he pitched his freshman year.

Tim Williamson '83 said Coach Fitzgerald told him he had the potential to be the best outfielder Newman had ever seen. "At the time, I believed him," he said. "And I started catching every ball, because I was 'the best outfielder Newman's ever had.' I'm not even sure he believed that, but he knew I needed to believe that. He was so intense and passionate about succeeding and winning."

Coach Fitzgerald's first basketball championships were 1977 and 1978. During one game in those winning years, the Greenies were losing to Country Day at halftime. Coach Fitz called his boys into the locker room, where it was assumed he would throw a fit, as he usually did, and start throwing things. Instead, he said in calm voice, "I don't think you boys understand how important this game is to the rest of your life." Coach Tuohy's son, Sean '78, was listening, and went back on the court and scored "about 600 points," Mr. Lewis said with a laugh. Newman won. In 1982, the *Absinthe* asked Coach Fitzgerald to name his favorite cartoon character. He said, "Road Runner — he always wins."

"He taught me lessons of achieving goals and work ethic and discipline and how to work with others and not be selfish," said Keith Miller '79. "Getting screamed at and working that hard — I don't think I'd have any kind of discipline without that. You're with teachers a semester; you're with a coach all year, all summer, for four years. He taught me to take a chance."

While he savors the memory of winning teams, Coach Fitzgerald said his favorite memories are of individual players, often in their darker hours, when they have needed him the most. "I have had some fantastic relationships with players. I would like to think that I brought some passion to what I do. I would like to think that some of the kids have caught on to the fact that it's okay to be passionate about some things."

Even those who didn't play basketball loved Coach Fitz. "He was my favorite teacher," said Lisa Lupin '86. "He taught earth science in the Middle School and he was just hilarious. And he really cared."

Gerald Williams '81 speaks for many when he says, "He was a model of leadership and integrity. I wouldn't be the man I am today without Tony Reginelli and him pouring into my life."

Girls' varsity sports are a modern phenomenon at Newman, beginning only in the late 1970s, but girls were playing basketball against each other as early as the 1910s. By 1922, they had well-organized intramural teams, Green and Orange, that played each other in various sports until varsity teams organized in the 1980s. Occasionally, they would play other schools, but it was never anything formal. As early as 1912, they played and beat a Jefferson Parish school. "The girls played a fast and interesting game," the *Pioneer* said.

Intramural sports were run by the Girls' Athletic Committee beginning around 1950. Some aspects of the GAC would be hooted at by today's female athletes: it used to stage an annual fashion show sponsored by Maison Blanche, whose president was Isidore Newman II. But when they weren't parading in the latest fashions, girls of that era were playing tennis, badminton and softball, running track and field and swimming. In the sixties, Newman offered thirteen different intramural sports for girls.

The gym teacher for the latter part of the GAC's history was Bobbie van der Giessen, who took over for Laura Chauvin. Born in Holland, she wore golf skirts to school every day, tried to introduce field hockey and liked to say "Run pretty!" to the girls running track. She was head of the girls' physical education department until 1977, when Mr. Cotonio named Claude "Boo" Mason head of both physical education and athletics for girls and boys. She retired in 1984. In Mrs. van der Giessen's day, the Orange team was made up of girls in grades seven, nine and eleven, and they played the Green team, with girls from grades eight, ten and twelve. The team with the most points at the end of a season would win the Green-Orange trophy. "The intramural program was fantastic," said Stephanie Bruno '70.

*We did volleyball, basketball, swimming and a kind of bizarre version of track and field. There was an odd event called 'softball catch and throw' where you*

TOP LEFT: *Volleyball, 1954, when it was an intramural sport for girls.* TOP RIGHT: *Girls played basketball against each other, and occasionally against other schools, until varsity sports began debuting in the late 1970s. Here, a group of basketball players in the 1960s.* BOTTOM LEFT: *Newman softball players, 1956.*

*literally stood on the basketball court, one girl on one side and one on the other, and they counted how many times you could toss the ball back and forth.*

A 1964 Greenie story confirms this: "The so-called 'track meet', which would hardly be recognized as such either by the ancient Greeks or the male members of the Newman student body, included such peculiar events as throwing softballs and baseballs for distance, and shooting baskets for one minute."

And they played what Ms. Bruno remembers as "a very archaic form of basketball. There were six on a side, four on one end and guards on the other end and you could not cross the center line. So you had to dribble to the center line and pass. But we were very, very competitive. It was serious."

The one thing girls competed in on a state level was swimming. The first interschool swim meet was in 1949. From 1959 to 1963, they won the Valencia Club swim meet against girls from such schools as McGehee's and Country Day. They placed third in the state in 1962; in 1963, the team, called "the Valiant Five," won the state title. They won again in 1964. In 1970, they set the state record for the 400 freestyle relay.

There were other small advances: in 1965, the girl athletes were invited to the annual Dads Club athletic banquet. But as late as 1969, girls' sports were still touted as primarily useful for improving poise and posture.

In the story of how girls' varsity sports came into being at Newman, Joanne Skertich could be called an unlikely hero. The woman who made volleyball Newman's most successful sport didn't even play the game as a child, nor had she ever coached before organizing Newman's first team. A New Orleans native, she majored in physical education at the University of New

Orleans because "that's where the boys were. I had no intentions of teaching. I went to school because I didn't want to work." And, she added, "I always wanted to be an athlete, I always tried out, but I never made the team. I was really small."

When she first came to Newman in 1974, Mrs. Skertich taught intramurals with Mrs. van der Giessen after school. She remembers the uncomfortable red and white and blue and white uniforms the girls had to wear, and a small interschool competition called the Ivy League.

In 1977, the girls began agitating to form a varsity volleyball team, and they asked Mrs. Skertich to be their coach. "I said, 'I have no idea how to do that,'" she said. Mr. Mason and Mr. Cotonio were very supportive of the idea, as volleyball was being played at other private schools. The team started off slowly, playing only five games a season. But by the time the Palaestra opened in 1981, it had become very popular. "I sat with Billy Fitzgerald every day getting advice," Mrs. Skertich recalled. "And I'd talk to my girlfriend at McGehee's, who was the volleyball coach there. We'd go over X's and O's on the phone while we cooked dinner for our families. I'd go to clinics. It took me a really long time to figure all this out."

But it didn't take long at all to figure out she'd found her place. "What I liked was being with the kids," she said. "They didn't care if I knew anything. They were so excited. I went in and said I don't have a clue, but I'll try. It was addicting. I didn't want to let them down."

She not only tried, she succeeded. Since winning their first state championship in 1985, the Greenie girls have won more than a dozen state championships. "At some point, we had more banners than Billy Fitzgerald," Mrs. Skertich said. "That was funny, since he was my mentor. Many years, we've been ranked number one or two in the state. And I'm talking number

# Volleyball Team Sets A Precedent With State Title

**Front Row:** Jessica McFaddin, Catherine McCarthy, Laurie Conway, Lisa Lupin, Ellen Hennessy, Martha White. **Back Row:** Boo Christy, Lizzie Lane, Kate Ballard, Paula Claverie (co-captain), Natalie Zellner (co-captain), Stephanie Cross, Emily Marrero, Coach Joanne Skertich.

*The volleyball team won its first state championship in 1985. As of 2003, the girls' volleyball team had fourteen state championships, more than any other Newman team.*

one against all the schools. It's really great from my standpoint to watch the girls get respect, to watch them achieve."

"She put the volleyball in my hand in third grade, and that was kind of it," said Meg Fitzgerald Colado '92, Coach Fitzgerald's daughter who played on three state championship teams at Newman and now coaches volleyball at the University of Central Florida.

> *That dictated the rest of my life. She was pretty remarkable. She understood the concept of team and team cohesiveness and team building light years ahead of other people. Even without a talented team, she could mold the girls and could motivate players to think about something other than themselves. I'm trying to learn to develop half the patience she has. She was the glue that kept us together.*

Elizabeth Conway Philipson '83, who was on the first volleyball team to make it to the state playoffs, remembers the pink polo socks they wore and how Mrs. Skertich would try to make the girls train with weights. "We just laughed," she said. "This was before the exercise craze." But they were serious about winning. "We beat Country Day one time and we were so excited, we stayed out all night," she said.

The rise of volleyball ushered in the modern era for girls' sports at Newman. In the eighties, girls began competing in varsity soccer, swimming, basketball, tennis, softball and track. Today, there are almost as many girls' teams as there are boys' teams; some years, there have been more. Mrs. Skertich said she was fortunate to have the administration behind her, and fortunate for the equal attention it has given to girls' athletics. "I don't think many schools can say that," she said. In 2002, Mrs. Skertich stopped coaching and became an assistant admission director. That year, the Newman Board of Governors voted to name the arena in the Palaestra the Fitzgerald/Skertich Arena. At the announcement, Newman parent and former trustee Joseph Henican said:

"Joanne Skertich is the best I have ever seen at getting kids to understand their roles on the team, to accept those roles and to get their parents to understand and accept those roles, even when that role is not as star of the team."

As the girls began their domination of the volleyball court, the boys began playing winning football. Since the eighties, the boys have had only one losing football season. The early nineties were especially remarkable years in Newman athletics, producing not one but several professional athletes. The most famous are the Manning boys, sons of former Saints quarterback Archie Manning. Eli '99 went on to be a star on the Ole Miss team; Peyton '94 played winning ball at the University of Tennessee and then signed with the Indianapolis Colts, and Cooper '92 was a star quarterback at Newman, and was Peyton's wide receiver when the younger Manning was a sophomore. "They were in a class by themselves," Coach Reginelli said. "You gotta get up early in the morning to think about what Peyton is thinking. He could out-work and out-think anyone. He was a student of the game. Peyton has so much leadership ability and he expresses it on the field."

And there were others. Omar Douglas '90 played football for Minnesota and then signed with the New York Giants. Randy Livingston '93 was considered the greatest basketball player Newman ever had, and perhaps the best the state had ever seen. He was a two-time All-American who won the Naismith Award as the national high school player of the year in 1993. In 1991, the basketball team won the state title for the first time since 1978. After the game, Peter Finney of the *Times-Picayune* said Randy Livingston "might be the finest fifteen-year-old player in the United States." He continued his career at LSU, and despite many injuries, went pro. He became a guard for the New Orleans Hornets in 2002.

In the fall of 1990, Coach Fitzgerald's son, William Edmond Fitzgerald Jr. '90 was named All-District, All-State and All-Metro in basketball, and was named male athlete of the year in Orleans Parish by the *Times-Picayune*, as well as male athlete of the metro area. The same year, Kathryn-McColl Simons '90 was named female athlete of the year in Orleans Parish. Fifteen out of sixteen Newman varsity teams played in state playoffs in 1989–90.

It might sound as though sports were threatening to overshadow academics, but that was never the case. "It's fun, and the kids want to be part of it," Coach Reginelli said. "It involves the school spirit. But I don't think sports should be placed before academics."

Coach Reg is part-time now, having scaled back in the early nineties after back and knee surgeries. "I can not do what I did before. You get close to seventy, and hey, it's not easy to get up in the morning." His daughter, Gaynell Reginelli Garey '80, now has a daughter at Newman. "That's what keeps me coming back here — to see my grandchild come here, and to go in the cafeteria and see kids whose parents I coached."

Winning has become almost expected from Newman teams. In 1999, the girls' soccer team won state for the first

*Coach Frank Gendusa with the girls' basketball team.*

time. In the spring of 2000, the boys won their first baseball state championship. In 1998–1999 and again in 2000–2001, Newman took home six state championships. Newman has won every Ford Cup, given annually since 1998 in each of the five Louisiana divisions. The girls have been the state swimming champions for five years in a row and have won eight out of the last nine volleyball titles.

So, is it something in the water at 1903 Jefferson Avenue?

"It's important to be faster, taller, stronger," Darryl Berger said. "But it's also important to have determination, team spirit, unity and basic smarts. Plus, we have great coaches."

*A scrapbook of modern-day athletics at Newman.*

# ON COACH ED "SKEETS" TUOHY

*BY ROBERT LANE '64*

*Bob Lane was a star basketball player at Newman, playing on three championship teams. He went to Davidson College on a basketball scholarship. From there, he has led an intellectually challenging and varied life. He attended the University of Chicago's divinity school and then earned a law degree at Stanford University. He practiced law in California and Maine until 1983, when he went back to school, obtaining an M.A. in English from Brandeis University and then a Ph. D. from Duke University. He taught English for almost ten years, all the while becoming increasingly interested in community theater. Today, he is an acting teacher in the Bay Area of San Francisco, and he is working to repeal the Patriot Act and prevent any other infringements on Americans' civil rights. He lives in Pleasanton with his wife, Sue, and their cat, Watson.*

COACH TUOHY HELPED US PLAY FOR FUN and win at the same time. You always had the feeling he was on your side, not, like my college coach, as if he was trying to beat effort out of unwilling, ungrateful players. We won a lot of games just because he was a better coach.

That's not modesty, because we played teams that had a lot of good athletes on them and won. We scrimmaged St. Augustine, and they were hands down the superior team athletically, but we more than held our own. Coach Tuohy inspired

you so that you wanted to hustle and work your fanny off, because it was fun, and winning was fun.

But I learned a lot more than just about how to win basketball games from him. Playing basketball helped me grow up. I learned how to take responsibility, what it means to lead, how to deal with failure, how to work and love doing it, how to be humble and confident, how to get along with teammates, some of whom I didn't spend any time with off the court. Personally, I learned how to take what I have and develop it, and I tasted the joy that goes with that. I learned just how much I could do. I learned what "heart" is, and how to be fully engaged in the moment. I learned how to find myself by losing it in that "zone."

I still think of him, some weeks almost every day. In his presence I shone. That's a priceless gift to give someone. And it wasn't always the joy of sharing success. Among the most meaningful moments in our relationship was when we lost the state championship when I was a sophomore. That was how we thought of it (we lost in the semifinals in Shreveport). He got us together in the hotel room. We had not prepared (mentally) for the game and deserved to lose. Whatever he said, what he was doing was forgiving us and telling us to forgive ourselves. And the last thing he did was he had us shout as loudly as we could, together, "SHIT!!!" It helped me get over the failure, and my part in that failure, and move on. I was back in the gym on Monday and worked hard all year and we went undefeated the next year and won the championship.

The other incident was my senior year. Coming off that

undefeated season, I think we — I — thought the wins would just come naturally. They didn't. We really struggled in December. The worst was in late December when we lost a tournament in Lake Charles. We didn't even score in the third quarter and Coach, rightly, chewed us out after the game because we weren't playing up to our potential. Back at the hotel I went to his room and he held me while I cried and we talked about what needed to happen. He was very gentle and never said it, but I knew I had to step up.

The next week we worked hard, but lost in the Lutcher Tournament to St. Amant, a team we would play five times that year, the last time in the state finals. We won three and they won two, the other one on our home court. This time Coach didn't chew us out. He said we worked hard and he was proud of the effort we showed, that we would get other chances to play them, and that we had nothing to be ashamed of. He knew the difference. So we trusted him completely to let us know how we were doing.

Though we lost one of our starters to a badly sprained ankle, we went on to beat St. Amant in a playoff for the district title and then for the state title. The reason was simple: we put our hats in the ring (a favorite phrase of Coach Tuohy's). We stopped acting like spoiled champions and started playing like we just wanted to be as good as we could be. The wins followed.

The guidance Coach Tuohy gave all of us, the love he showed me — that was what basketball at Newman meant to me.

*Randy Livingston '93.*

Alice in Wonderland, *in 1984.*

# CHAPTER ELEVEN

# The End of an Era

The school was always a monument to Isidore
Newman. Now it is a monument to Teddy.
One man gave it money. The other gave it new life.

HERMAN KOHLMEYER JR. '49

On January 28, 1986, the space shuttle Challenger, carrying six astronauts and the first civilian ever to be launched into space, exploded in mid-air seventy-three seconds after liftoff. But that is not what Isidore Newman School remembers about that day. Just hours after the news of that national tragedy began to dominate the air waves, Teddy Cotonio died in a car wreck on his way to a Newman basketball game.

One of Mr. Cotonio's trademarks was his love of game. He attended just about every athletic competition he could ram into his schedule. His wife, Asta, used to be irritated by how vigorously he cheered. "He yelled and screamed at all the games and I would fuss," she said. "I thought he was too demonstrative. But he was always there to make up. He'd bring me camellias and say he was sorry."

He cheered on the burgeoning girls volleyball team in the new Palaestra, he was a fixture on the sidelines of the new football field, and he drove his station wagon to away games, often toting parents and students with him. It was on just such a journey that his life was cut short, and an era at Newman abruptly ended. Genie Everett McCloskey '65 was with Mr. Cotonio in the car, and remembers every detail:

LEFT: *Newman chorus directed by Marilyn Bernard performed on Founder's Day, 1986.*

*His son Tony was in my son Sean's class. They were sophomores in 1985–86, and my son P.J. was a senior. It was January 28, kind of the thick of basketball season. We had a game in Port Sulphur, which is down at the mouth of the river. And to get there you had to go on just a two-lane highway. A bunch of us would drive together, and on this occasion, Teddy was going to drive. He had a big LTD station wagon, a black one with that wood floofy trim stuff. Also in the car were David and Marlis Perlis, and Kay Simons — our three sons were best friends from the very beginning. And two cheerleaders, Katie Marrero '88 and Virginia Hearin '88 were in the back.*

*So we're driving along, and we were early. We were going to the J.V. game because Tony and Sean would be playing in the J.V. game. And along the way is this restaurant called Sig's. Teddy loved to eat, loved a good meal, so we decided to stop at Sig's. I was not too thrilled because I was going to watch my children play basketball. Other Newman families who were on the road decided to stop also.*

*Anyway it was a lovely meal, and we got back in the car. David was in the front passenger seat, and behind the driver was Kay and then me and then Marlis. I always had my camera with me so it was sitting on my lap. David and Teddy were talking and Kay and Marlis were talking and I was looking straight ahead. And I saw this one kind of light coming to us and I thought it was a motorcycle. Well it wasn't. It was a car passing another car. It hit us head-on, and particularly on the driver's side, and totally crunched the steering wheel into Teddy. I was so disoriented, I got out*

*of the car apparently asking for Shannon [her daughter, class of '92]. Because Shannon was supposed to have gone with us. The rescue people came right away and they had to get this thing, this wrenching jaw thing to pry him out. They took us all to this little bitty hospital, a little rural, one-story hospital. And I go in this door — my hand is all mangled and I look across the hall, and I see Teddy, and I remember asking the nurse or somebody, "Well how's Teddy?" They said, "He's gone."*

*Somehow the people at the basketball game started realizing we had never made it. Kay was really badly hurt, so they took her back to the city. David was cut by flying glass and Marlis had a back injury. My injury was basically my hand and bruising around my heart. We were all pretty banged up. I wasn't wearing a seatbelt — this was 1986.*

*I ended up coming back in an ambulance. I must have been in the hospital three or four days because I totally missed the funeral. The funeral was at Bultman. Apparently it was like a head of state died, the crowd was just so unbelievable. I don't know, I missed it.*

*When I went back, it was Founder's Day. And we had it in the Palaestra, and it was really hard.*

Newman went about the grim business of mourning the loss. School was closed on January 30 and most people went to Bultman Funeral Home to pay their respects. Later there was a mass at Holy Name; several faculty members served as pallbearers. He was buried not far from Isidore Newman in Metairie Cemetery. "I remember this guy from two grades above me sobbing in my arms," said Sabrina Forman Pilant '88. Founder's Day was ten days after the accident, and it became a memorial

*After Teddy Cotonio's death in January 1986, some members of the boys' basketball team wore black ribbons emblazoned with their headmaster's initials, "TCIII," on their uniforms. Photo by Kurt Mutschler. Copyright 2003 The Times-Picayune Publishing Co., all rights reserved. Used with permission of the Times-Picayune.*

for Mr. Cotonio. For the rest of basketball season, players wore black ribbons bearing their headmaster's initials — TCIII.

For a lot of people, the loss was deeply personal. Mr. Cotonio was friends with many Newman families. He was the godfather to one of Coach Billy Fitzgerald's children, for example. "It was devastating for the school, but it was also a family tragedy," said Meg Fitzgerald Colado '92.

"Teddy was part of who I am," Coach Fitzgerald said. "He was much more than a mentor and a father figure. A lot of my passion is his passion. During that time, some of the players I was coaching were having similar relationships with Teddy. My pain was their pain. It was a difficult time for all of us."

Of course the loss was felt most deeply by Mr. Cotonio's wife and his two sons, Keighley and Tony, who were eleven and fifteen years old at the time and attending Newman. Mrs. Cotonio takes great comfort in what she heard from a paramedic who was with her husband at the scene of the wreck: "His last words were that he had made his peace with God."

For many people, the center, the very essence of Newman, had died. "My first reaction was, 'I'm quitting,'" Sheila Collins said. Fortunately for Newman, she did not. Kitty Greenberg said a parent told her she was afraid to come to the school after Teddy died, for fear it would no longer be there. "He literally transformed the school," said Herman Kohlmeyer Jr. soon after he died. "In his ten years as headmaster, Teddy changed the face of the school and gave it a new heart. He pushed, bullied, bargained and wheedled with his board to expand the plant." At the end of the year, the *Absinthe* carried a memorial to the headmaster: "Mr. Cotonio was a dreamer, with great plans for the school. Mr. Cotonio was Newman personified."

Lisa Lupin '86 remembers how sad commencement was. "He had been our headmaster almost the whole time we were in school, but he wasn't there to do the speeches or give out the diplomas." P.J. McCloskey '86 was chosen by his class to give the commencement speech. He spoke of the headmaster:

> *Mr. Cotonio. The man somehow really did have a heart bigger than his body. Not only did he know all of our names, he knew all of our strengths. Our successes, whether big or small, always received a chuckle or a smile from this good-humored man. The chuckles were his way of telling himself that he knew we would succeed. But if we failed, he willingly offered us his insights and gave us new directions, so we would not have to be denied again. We are fortunate to have been part of his extended family.*

*Michael Lacopo, Newman's headmaster from 1987 to 1993.*

Meanwhile, Newman had to get back to the business of being a school. Jonathan Hutchison, principal of the Upper School, was named acting headmaster. In the fall of 1987, Michael Lacopo took over as Mr. Cotonio's permanent replacement. The South Bend, Indiana native was educated at Columbia College, Fairfield University and Middlebury College, earning his bachelor's and master's degrees in English. From 1956 to 1958, he interrupted his undergraduate career to serve in the Marine Corps. He began working in independent education as an English teacher and a coach. He then worked in college admissions, serving as Associate Director and Director of Admissions for Columbia College, the undergraduate divi-

sion of Columbia University. After nine years at Columbia, he held several administrative positions at Horace Mann School in New York. He and his wife, Charlotte, had four children, all out of high school by the time he arrived in New Orleans. Mr. Lacopo was an athlete; tennis was his favorite sport, but he also enjoyed basketball, hiking and running.

During his tenure, some very important things happened at Newman, including the recruitment of top-notch teachers, an increased focus on bringing in more minority students and the establishment of Summerbridge. "He recruited teachers from all over the country," said David Stone '57. "He brought in some young teachers of tremendous talent."

Alan Philipson '56, who was chairman of the Board of Governors from 1989 to 1992, said those were the years when Newman began diversifying in earnest: "It was not the easiest move. But it was a necessary move. And today, it is undoubtedly a better school thanks to Mike's efforts."

The late eighties were a time of modernizing for Newman. In 1986, as the New Orleans economy hit rock bottom thanks to an oil bust, the school introduced a yearlong course for seniors that would dramatically alter the way they learned. Called Humanities, it aimed to bridge the gap between science, art, literature, history, math and economics through the study of an era in history. One of the first eras studied was World War I and its aftermath. The course is designed to teach students to think for themselves, to respect differing opinions and to introduce them to intellectual inquiry and collaboration. It is one of the most challenging and rewarding classes at Newman today.

"Humanities was by far the most important class we took," said Sabrina Forman Pilant. "We studied 1890 to 1930. I didn't understand the concept at first, but then it all came together.

CLOCKWISE FROM TOP LEFT: *George Wolfe, Newman art teacher from 1965 to 1996. Art students from the class of 1987. Latin Club, 1989. George Wolfe, pictured here with students making foam figures.*

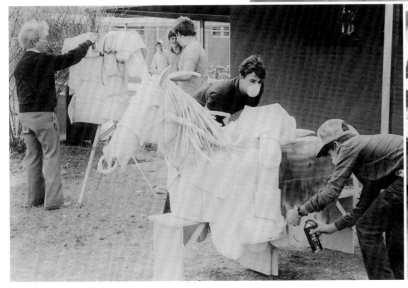

*ABOVE: McLain Forman and daughter Sabrina Forman Pilant '88 at Homecoming, 1987.* LEFT: *A life-size, Wright brothers-era airplane model, created by Ian Alexander '94 as his final project in Humanities. Photo by Kim D. Johnson. Copyright 2003 The Times-Picayune Publishing Co., all rights reserved. Used with permission of the* Times-Picayune.

We studied the Impressionist painters, Bauhaus architecture and jazz. We had movie nights. We read Kafka. It was amazing. I did my final project on Newcomb pottery. The format was so much more like college."

Newman attracted the media to Lupin Field in 1994 for one student's Humanities project. Ian Alexander '94 created a life-size model of a Wright Brothers-era airplane using a sketch from a 1915 edition of Popular Mechanics. In 2002–2003, the students studied the turn of the twentieth century; Bobby Ragsdale '03 built an actual still that with a little tinkering could have produced moonshine. Two of his classmates studied jazz and Klezmer music and recorded their own improvised arrangement combining the two styles. "The Humanities program is vital to the school's curriculum," said Kate Barron, who chairs the department. "It provides good preparation for college learning, according to our students; it does provoke connections between ideas in different disciplines, and it brings the class together." Everyone presents their final projects to the whole senior class and later to their parents at a Humanities dinner in the spring.

In 1987, Mr. Lacopo relaxed the already relaxed dress code. Students were now allowed to wear jeans and untucked shirts, and they no longer had to wear socks or belts. Mr. Lacopo also succeeded in winning support for a Lower School uniform. An outcry from parents forced him to delay his decision in 1988, but by 1989, the Board approved it.

After agitation from students, the girls in the Homecoming Court began a new tradition. Instead of being escorted onto the football field by alumni, they would walk out with their own fathers. Marriott, the hotel corporation, took over management of the cafeteria. By 1989, the annual fund had reached almost $600,000 and enrollment was 1,140. Students

207

was most closely identified," said David Stone '57, who was chairman of the Board of Governors.

*Teddy conceived this building, and begged, cajoled, and connived to get it approved and built. With the support and superb leadership of board chairman Sydney Besthoff, who shared with Teddy the role of construction superintendent, it was planned and completed. It stands now as an embodiment of Teddy's vision and as a monument to his ambition for the school.*

As the decade drew to a close, English teacher Jay Altman spoke with Mr. Lacopo about a student teaching program he had seen in San Francisco called Summerbridge. It had two objectives: to prepare disadvantaged youths to enter strong high schools, and to encourage students from top high schools and colleges to consider teaching as a career. The headmaster was intrigued.

*Summerbridge students and student teachers.*

were hanging out at the Boot, where, said Michael Stone '91, "the same seven songs always seemed to be playing."

On May 15, 1987, the Palaestra was dedicated to Mr. Cotonio. "It is singularly appropriate that we meet today to dedicate to Teddy Cotonio the building with which he

*LEFT: Jay Altman, an English teacher who brought the idea of Summerbridge to Newman. RIGHT: Hunter Pierson '97.*

In early 1990, the school announced that a tuition-free, six-week tutoring program for New Orleans public school students would begin that summer. Fifth and sixth graders from public schools would be taught by high school and college students from Newman and elsewhere. Funding for Summerbridge initially came from a $25,000 gift from the Lupin Foundation. It was the second school in the nation to establish the program, and it was an immediate success with both the student teachers and the students themselves. "That was the hardest job I ever had," said Geeta Karnik '98.

*You have to have lesson plans and create activities. It was like a twenty-four-hour-a-day job. But it's wonderful how the kids respond to the personal attention they get. They are used to having so many kids in a class. At Summerbridge, they get a good edge — in study skills, organization and learning to love learning. It's a great two-way street. My eyes were opened so much. You learn about their backgrounds and the areas of town they live in — it was sometimes shocking. You get a perspective outside of Jefferson Avenue.*

Hunter Pierson '97 taught with Summerbridge for three summers, and said it changed his perspective on education in general and Newman in particular. "Newman has a tendency to be very insular, and it reached out to the community around it, and made a decision to be invested in the community," he said. "I feel so fortunate to have had a top flight education but also to have been endowed with a sense of duty, to have fallen in love with education enough to want to pass it along." After graduating from Harvard, Mr. Pierson became a teacher himself, and today is the executive director of the San Francisco Bay Area region of Teach for America. "People ask, 'What do you want to

*Michael Walker '99, a Summerbridge student who became a Newman student, and Keith Miller '79, who befriended Mr. Walker.*

do in ten years?'" he said. "I say I would love to create a Newman that's tuition-free."

Many Summerbridge children have transferred to Newman. Michael Walker '99 came to Newman in seventh grade, after two years in Summerbridge. "Summerbridge was really idyllic," he said. "I grew up in an all-black background in the inner-city of New Orleans; Summerbridge was my first encounter with people outside my race. And it opened up the possibility of learning, and learning in an exciting way with energetic young people. It was a great experience."

Mr. Walker grew up with a mother who he says "had a rough life." He never really knew his father. He lived with rela-

209

tives, sometimes with a grandfather, sometimes with an aunt. When he was encouraged by Summerbridge administrators to apply to Newman, he did, and was accepted, with financial aid. But getting in wasn't the hard part. "Newman presented a bunch of challenges for me," he said.

*Everyone was more or less wealthy and my background was humble and meager. I was dealing with that and with my different ethnicity — really everyone in my class was white except two or three. I was isolated. And a lot of these people had grown up together, so here I am the new guy. So I was trying to find my place at Newman, and deal with the academics.*

Mr. Walker joined the Middle School basketball team, and that was when things began to change for him.

*I found my place, he said. I found it to be challenging — to have a sport on top of academics — but I found a community I could really trust. It allowed me to open myself up to a lot of people at Newman. I played in high school too. So at that point I had a good core group of people I could trust and call my friends — even though we did not hang out regularly.*

Keith Miller '79, who met Mr. Walker through his involvement with Summerbridge, said he was "a little, meek, shy kid" when he first came to Newman. "I started to go to basketball games with him, and then I asked if he wanted to stay with me on a weekend here and there. Then it kind of developed; he opened up." When Mr. Walker's grandfather died, Mr. Miller

took the boy under his wing; Mr. Walker lived with Mr. Miller for several years, until he graduated. "He's such an unbelievable spirit," said Mr. Miller. "I learned so much from him, it's frightening. I didn't realize when I first met him how smart he was and his innate ability to work and listen. And not one time did I have to get him to do his homework."

Meanwhile, Michael Walker blossomed. When he graduated, he was named most esteemed classmate by his fellow seniors. "Newman was a turning point," Mr. Walker said. "Racism didn't go away and dealing with my economic background didn't go away, but I came to accept people for who they are. And I realized we are all flawed people and I don't hold a grudge because someone is white or has money." Mr. Walker went on to Washington University in St. Louis, Missouri, and then to a job in the business management department at Boeing.

Today, Newman holds a six-week Summerbridge session each summer and there is a year-round tutoring program. Many schools have followed Newman's example; there are now dozens of Summerbridge programs throughout the country.

In 1993, Mike Lacopo left Newman, and New Orleans. "Working to broaden the reach of the school, Mike expanded its character," said Lewis Cobbs, then head of the English department, in a *Newman News* article. "As we embrace the neighborhoods from which Newman has not traditionally aimed to attract students, we enlarge our sphere of service; we become an independent school of and for New Orleans — and a school that all of New Orleans will support and enrich in the future."

RIGHT: *Class of 2010 in first grade, 1999.*

# IT'S NOT EASY BEIN' A GREENIE

### BY TRAVIS LEBLANC '95

*Upon graduating from Newman, Travis LeBlanc completed his undergraduate studies with honors in philosophy, politics and economics at Princeton and Oxford universities. He received a master's degree in Public Administration from Harvard University's John F. Kennedy School of Government and a law degree from Yale Law School, where he championed both Yale's Moot Court and the American Bar Association's National Appellate Advocacy Competition. He has worked in the New York office of Cravath, Swaine & Moore; the Los Angeles office of Skadden, Arps, Slate, Meagher & Flom; the Washington office of Williams & Connolly, and the Appellate Section of the Civil Rights Division of the United States Department of Justice. Awarded a Kennedy Fellowship, Travis is currently studying international law at Cambridge University in England. He will return to the United States next year to serve as a law clerk to the Honorable Stephen Reinhardt of the United States Court of Appeals for the Ninth Circuit.*

I AM SURE MANY OF YOU at one time or another have asked that eternal Newman question: what exactly is a Greenie?

Allow me to confess that I have spent more than a decade pondering this. Having learned the value of a dictionary in Kate Barron's senior English composition class, I thought I might begin my inquiry into the meaning of "Greenie" by looking it up in my handy Webster's. To my dismay, I was able to find entries for Greenie's homophonic twin "greeny" and its superlative cousin "greenier," but I was unable to find any entry for the dearly beloved we now celebrate.

Having no luck with the dictionary — or any of Mr. Prescott's hardbound reference materials for that matter — I decided to Google the term. The search engine informed me that there were 37,500 websites referring to the word. A cursory survey of the results initially directed me to a website for the Greenie Genie (self-proclaimed as the "world's greatest divot tool"), but the overwhelming majority of the hits were to websites promoting environmental activism, Ralph Nader's Green party, and last but certainly not least, Greenies' dog biscuits and treats.

Alas, all was not lost. One of my results brought me to thesaurus.com where I was surprised to learn that Greenie is synonymous with a "fledgling, newcomer, or recruit." While such a characterization may have been apropos in 1903, certainly no one would think of Newman School as a fledgling today.

Ultimately, I'm not sure the real significance of a school's nickname can be found in a dictionary. As I see it, a school's nickname is more than a rallying cry before a football game. It is a term of endearment that expresses the common and shared experience we all have as members of the Newman family. As such, it is an intergenerational personification, not of one of us or even a majority of us, but of all of us — past and present. Unlike Ben Franklin's falcon or Jesuit's blue jay, the Greenie takes on the image that we make of it. The beauty of the Greenie truly is in the eye of its beholder.

To be a Greenie is to live a certain lifestyle. It is living with a core set of values that Newman instills in its students. When financier and philanthropist Isidore Newman founded the Isidore Newman Manual Training School in 1903, he wrote, "For years it has been the desire of my heart to do something for this city and state which have made me what I am. I have my reward in this school." Uncle Izzy did not just want to give students skills that they could use while they were in school; he envisioned an educational institution that would train them for life. He wanted the graduates of Newman to be trained with the skills necessary to do the work of the community in which they lived. The school was to have a public mission.

While the school has modernized its education to meet the demands of the twenty-first century, it has stayed true to its founding idea. It continues to manually train students in core values that are essential to the intellectual and moral development of its students. When I reflect on my experience as a Newman student, I am heartened by just how much of a difference Newman has made and continues to make in my life. Newman instilled in me a commitment to my community, recognition of responsibility, and a sense of honor and integrity. Despite having no community service requirement, Newman students share a strong commitment to serving others and the city, whether as a Lower School aide, an Allen or Lewis schools volunteer, or a Summerbridge teacher. Newman encouraged us

to take responsibility for our actions and our lives. Freedom comes as we age, but it only travels with responsibility and the integrity to exercise it honorably. Those values are not inscribed on a wall or taught in a special class; they are omnipresent.

But I don't mean to portray Newman as perfect, as not needing to evolve. For years, Newman has attempted to promote open dialogue among its students. As diversity becomes one of Newman's core values, such a dialogue becomes even more important. The school will continue to be successful only if the community respects and cherishes the contribution diverse individuals add to the whole. Each individual represents only a part of that Greenie spirit that we all share together.

Newman gave me core values, but the challenge is actually living them. As its mission statement concludes, "Newman instills in each student the skills, attitudes, and ethics necessary for productive, lifelong learning." It was never all that challenging to participate in a school-sponsored community service project or to adhere to the honor code while at 1903 Jefferson Avenue. The real challenge, I have found, has come since I left those training grounds. It comes years later as I attempt to live a life that reflects the values Newman instilled in me. A life's commitment to participating in the community, taking responsibility for one's life and actions, respecting others, and living with a sense of honor and integrity is not nearly as easy in the "real world." With apologies to Kermit the Frog: It's Not Easy Bein' a Greenie!

# Philanthropy

ISIDORE NEWMAN'S 1902 GIFT endowing a manual training school for Jewish orphans set the tone for a century of generosity. Alumni, parents, friends and even teachers have funded dramatic campus expansions and upgrades, scholarships and teaching chairs.

It is tempting to name generous donors throughout Newman's first century, but the list would be a book in itself. One name, however, stands out: Freeman. The Freeman family has provided more support to Isidore Newman School than any other individual, family or foundation.

The family has been a part of Newman — and New Orleans — for almost a century. A.B. Freeman, who came to New Orleans in 1906, began building the family fortune with a local Coca-Cola bottling franchise. He used his financial success to begin a tradition of giving that his family enthusiastically continues. Freemans have contributed to New Orleans in ways too numerous to count, and they have been rewarded for their generosity and civic spirit; multiple Freemans have been kings and queens of Carnival and two, Rosa Keller Freeman and Richard West Freeman Sr., have received the *Times-Picayune's* prestigious Loving Cup, and they have received many awards and commendations for their devotion to the city. "They really have set the bar for philanthropy not only for Newman, but in the community," said Carol McCall, Newman's Director of Advancement. "I enjoy it," Louis Freeman says of his civic work. "I think it is incumbent upon anybody to try and make the community they live in a better place."

Louis Freeman and Richard West Freeman Jr., sons of Montine and Richard West Freeman, give time and money to countless causes. Richard is active in two of the family foundations — The RosaMary Foundation and The Ella West Freeman Foundation. Louis chairs the latter. The foundations give to New Orleans institutions and causes, especially those dealing with education and community development, such as Tulane University, the United Way, the Greater New Orleans Foundation, and of course, Isidore Newman School. "They give because they believe in the organizations, and they believe in making a difference, but they don't give for personal recognition," Mrs. McCall said.

Three of Judy and Louis Freeman's four children graduated from Newman — Dr. Laura Louise Freeman '81, Peter Freeman '85 and Virginia Freeman Rowan '87. Their son, Louis Freeman Jr., serves on the Board of Governors at Newman. The elder Louis now has grandchildren at the school and likes what he sees today. "I think the school is defined by the success of the students it produces and Newman has certainly done a good job of that. It's a challenging environment and offers a broad selection of extracurricular activities." Louis Freeman served on Newman's Board of Governors 1979–1986 and led the effort to create the Theodore Cotonio Chair in Humanities. Today, Louis is the chairman of Newman's Investment Committee. "For more than a decade, he has monitored the school's endowment," said Headmaster Scott McLeod. "And he has done an extraordinary job. Other schools

*RIGHT TOP: Freeman family members.*
*RIGHT BOTTOM: Class of 2008 present their newsletter to the Headmaster Scott Mcleod and Ben Rosen '50.*

have been hammered in the last three years with the downturn in the economy, but our returns place Newman in the top ten percent of comparable schools."

Richard Freeman was president of the family's Coca-Cola franchise when it was sold to Coca-Cola of Atlanta in the 1980s. Today he concentrates mainly on philanthropic and civic activities. He is a member of Tulane University's board; Louis is an emeritus member. His wife, Sandra, served on Newman's Board from 1971–1980.

Freemans and Kellers have been going to and supporting Newman for generations. Louis and Richard's father, Richard West Freeman, attended Newman, and all of his children attended. He had two sisters, Rosa Freeman Keller and Mary Freeman Wisdom, for whom the RosaMary Foundation is named. Rosa Freeman Keller, a noted New Orleans civil rights activist, attended Newman and graduated from Louise S. McGehee School; she and her husband, Chuck, were lifelong supporters of Newman, and she played a role in the school's 1968 integration. One of their three children, Charles Keller III '53, for whom the Charles Keller III Memorial Fine Arts Center is named, served on the Board of Governors until he died in 1979. His wife, Julie, served as treasurer of the board after his death. Charles's sisters are Newman alumni: Caroline Keller Loughlin '57 and Mary Keller Zervigon '56. Ashley Keller Nelson, Charles Keller's daughter, graduated in 1983.

Mary Freeman Wisdom '24 was married to William B. Wisdom, for whom the chair in English, one of the first two endowed chairs at Newman, is named. Mr. Wisdom, an advertising executive and a noted collector of rare books and manuscripts, graduated from Newman in 1917. The couple had three children, Betty Wisdom '48 and Adelaide Wisdom Benjamin, who attended Newman, and William B. Wisdom Jr. '54.

Of course, other names stand out as well. The largest single endowment fund, the Ana L. Rosen Scholarship Fund, was donated by Benjamin M. Rosen '50. Mr. Rosen, who had a twenty-year career as an analyst on Wall Street and started a venture capital fund in the early 1980s, has been interested in technology and computers for decades. He launched Lotus Development and by 1983 was serving as Chairman of Compaq Computer Corporation. He stepped down in the late nineties to pursue other interests. He received the Newman Distinguished Alumnus Award in 1992. The Ana L. Rosen Scholarship Fund is named for Mr. Rosen's mother.

*Carol Graves McCall '58, Newman's Director of Advancement.*

The names of other important donors grace buildings and public spaces all over campus — families such as the Bergers, the Besthoffs, the Gottesmans, the Heymanns, the Lupins, the Marcus Levys, the Orecks and the Sterns, to name just a few.

The most recent fundraising campaign — *Newman 2000* — raised an unprecedented $18.4 million. Today's endowment stands at $24 million, and the annual fund now generates about $750,000. Carol Graves McCall, who graduated from Newman in 1958, married Newman alumnus Mac McCall '54 and sent two children to Newman, Richard '86 and Barrett '83, has been director of development and advancement since 1978. She can remember when she was happy to raise $50,000 in a given year.

"You can run a great school without money — but not for long," Mr. McLeod said.

*Class of 2009 in Lower School.*

*A few days after September 11, 2001, the Newman community gathered on Michael Lupin Field for a moment of silence. Photo by Kate Elkins.*

# CHAPTER TWELVE

# A Bright Future in the Making

—◦◦◦—

*If Isidore Newman and Rabbi Isaac Leucht could come back and pay a visit, they'd be very pleased at what they saw.*

LOUIS FISHMAN '59

IT IS AUGUST 20, 2003 when the Newman faculty convenes to prepare for the new school year. It is still and hot, as it was in 1904 when the first faculty met in James Addicott's office before Newman's opening day. Now, there is air-conditioning, so the meeting does not have to be brief, and the group is so large it fills up bleachers and chairs on three sides of the Keller Center auditorium. Tom Rushing, Director of Academic Affairs, addresses the faculty. He begins by talking about two alumni, Michael Lewis '78 and Walter Isaacson '70, both of whom have books on *The New York Times* bestseller list. "How often does it happen that a single school has two prominent authors at the same time?" Mr. Rushing asks. Mr. Lewis's *Moneyball* is dedicated to Coach Billy Fitzgerald.

Mr. Rushing, who has been at Newman for more than thirty years, talks of a window he has noticed in the new Lower School; it offers a panoramic view of Newman's property and all its buildings, old and new. "It is a new spot, a new way to look at campus, one that shows where dreaming, hard work, flexibility, compromise, generosity and devotion to this place can take us."

Headmaster Scott McLeod is the last to speak to the faculty. He can be serious, and he

*LEFT: Class of 2009 with Headmaster Scott McLeod.*

*LEFT: Tom Rushing, Newman's Director of Academic Affairs, dressed up as Isidore Newman for the centennial celebration that took place on Lupin Field in September 2003. CENTER: Scott McLeod took over as interim headmaster in 1993. RIGHT: Susan Good is the first female chairman of Newman's Board of Governors.*

can be very funny, and sometimes it's hard to tell which is which. He concludes his speech with this:

"It has been my intention to continue to be head of this school for two more years. But some recent events may affect that decision."

The room grows very quiet.

"I have been approached about running for governor of California."

The room erupts into laughter, as this is the summer Californians are seeking to recall Governor Gray Davis, and more than one hundred candidates are vying to take his place. Someone asks Mr. McLeod if he is worried about taking on actor Arnold Schwarzenegger, a leading candidate. Mr. McLeod

says he plans to lose an arm wrestle with the Terminator and win sympathy votes from wimps everywhere. The room echoes with more laughter and applause.

Mr. McLeod then describes what Newman looks like in its hundredth year. There are 1,155 students in fourteen grades, and 272 adults. Tuition, which started at $50, is now almost $13,000 a year. Minorities comprise nineteen percent of the student body, and fewer than half the students come from Uptown homes. Thirty-six seniors — almost a third of the class — will be recognized in National Merit competition this year, more than in any high school in the state. The mean SAT score at Newman is 1311.

"And we're a nicer place," Mr. McLeod says. "We care

222

about each other more than we did ten years ago." Most people would attribute this change to Mr. McLeod himself.

Scott McLeod loves to hate New Orleans. His professed dislike of his adopted city may be a sly running joke — one of many he shares with colleagues and friends — but there is no doubt he misses his two grown daughters, who live in Palo Alto, California, as well as the climate and culture of California, where he lived for more than thirty years. This makes his decade in the Crescent City — he was only meant to stay a year — a tribute to Newman. For it is his love of the school that has kept him here.

When Scott McLeod first arrived from California in 1993 as interim headmaster, he was given two jobs: the first was to heal schisms among the staff. There were divisions among young and veteran faculty, and there were pay inequities to be straightened out. Mr. McLeod, who had been a headmaster at Cate School near Santa Barbara for nearly twenty years, made quick work of this first job.

The second task was to retool Newman's mission statement. For several months Mr. McLeod talked with students, faculty, trustees, alumni and parents, asking them to help him define what Newman wanted to be. Then he sat down and crafted the actual wording. He made the first sentence simple and powerful: "Newman values each individual." The last sentence is a clear road map for what students can expect: "Newman instills in each student the skills, attitudes, and ethics necessary for productive, lifelong learning."

In the ten years since it was created, the statement has informed everything Newman does. "It is a living, breathing part of the school," said Assistant Headmaster Joan Starr, who was hired by Mr. McLeod in 1995 as the school's first Assistant Headmaster. It has seeped into the very foundation of the

*Joan Starr, a Newman parent and trustee, became Assistant Headmaster in 1995.*

school, and become its rallying cry, its public persona, its mantra. "That is probably the biggest change I've made," Mr. McLeod said.

*It is where my imprint has been felt the most. This has always been a fine academic institution, it has always had a strong athletic program and the arts have always been good. But the school lacked heart. It was a school where kids could fall through the cracks. You had to be really good or really bad to stand out. Being average at Newman is still pretty good, and we weren't communicating that to a lot of the kids.*

Susan Good, who is chairman of the Board of Governors and mother to two Newman graduates, Jenny '97 and Jeffrey '01, said she noticed the extra personal attention. "Newman now looks at each kid, and finds out what sparks them," she

223

said. "They go so far as to teach organizational skills, such as how to organize your locker."

By the time Mr. McLeod finished his two assignments, a funny thing had happened: he had become attached to Newman. After decades spent teaching and administrating to older students, he fell in love with Newman's Lower School. "I was so invigorated by working in a school that had primary education," he said. "I began to appreciate that the really important learning isn't what happens in high school. What really matters is how you inculcate kids with an enthusiasm for learning, an excitement about being in school, at a very early age." The lure of working in a K-12 institution, combined with what he called "a two-man press" from trustees Jay Lapeyre and Philip Claverie, convinced Mr. McLeod to stay.

Scott McLeod was born in Wilkes-Barre, Pennsylvania in 1940, and grew up in Hatfield, Massachusetts, a small tobacco and onion town. His father ran a family manufacturing company, but always wanted to be a teacher. Mr. McLeod attended Deerfield Academy and Governor Dummer Academy, private boys' boarding schools, and graduated from Governor Dummer in 1958. He went on to Wesleyan University where he was captain of the lacrosse team, president of his fraternity, a reporter for the newspaper and an English major. He then earned a master's degree in teaching from Harvard in 1963 and landed his first teaching job in Hawaii. In 1965, he got a new job at Cate School, an all-boys boarding school in southern California, as an English teacher, dorm master and tennis coach. "I was hired over the phone," he said. He spent ten years as a teacher and later as an administrator, and discovered he was better at the latter. Meanwhile, he earned an Ed.D. from the University of Massachusetts. He was thirty-six years old when

*Newman's percussion ensemble, 2003.*

the position of headmaster opened, and he felt he was ready: "I was enthusiastic enough and naïve enough to think I could do it." He was hired, and remained in the position for eighteen years. "It was a wonderful run," he said. While he was headmaster, the school became coeducational, and it raised its national stature, becoming competitive with the more established eastern boarding schools. "That was pretty exciting," Mr. McLeod said.

But Cate was small — only 250 students in grades nine to twelve. "And eighteen years is a long time," Mr. McLeod said. "A boarding school is a twenty-four-hour-a-day, seven-days-a-week job. I'd gone through two marriages. It was taking a toll." So he decided he wanted to leave independent schools and find a small foundation to direct. Then he received two calls, one from a school in northern California looking for an interim headmaster, and one from an independent school in New Orleans — Newman. He chose Newman. "I figured if it's just for a year, why not go to a place that's very different?" said Mr. McLeod.

"He was hired as our interim, in a bit of an emergency, but we got great references," Mr. Lapeyre said. Mrs. Starr was a trustee on the search committee when the board hired Mr. McLeod for the permanent position. "The sentiment was, 'Don't let him go, we'll never find anybody else like him,'" she said. "Once he was in, the change was so extraordinary, from the very beginning. There's a real humanity and a kindness here now."

Dave Prescott remembers Mr. McLeod coming to the library when he first arrived to ask for copies of the *Absinthe*, so he could get to know who everyone was. "He was only the acting headmaster, but he wanted to know names," he said.

"He has brought to Newman a sensitivity and a gentleness toward the students that surpasses any before him," said Darryl Berger '65. "There is a genuine concern in the deepest part of his soul that the happiness of each kid is what really matters at Newman. Any kid left behind, unsuccessful, unfulfilled is a true failure."

Students noticed the change. "More was expected of teachers than just teaching," said Hunter Pierson '97. "You expected them to be devoted to the whole student, and they

*Children show their Newman pride.*

were. And they had an extreme amount of faith in our creativity."

Everyone seems taken with Mr. McLeod. "I adore Scott," said Linda Gottesman Baum, a trustee, a Newman parent, and an alumna from the class of 1967. "He's no-nonsense and he has such a nice way about him. And if you ask him something, he gives you a straight answer."

Mr. McLeod was fascinated by the challenge of creating a curriculum with continuity through fourteen years of education, and making it work in a population of more than 1,000 students and 150 faculty. Joellen Welch, who has taught fourth grade at Newman for twenty-eight years, said there is more dialogue now between the divisions; Lower School teachers meet with their colleagues from the Middle and Upper schools to discuss math instruction, for example.

225

After mending fences among the faculty and hammering out the mission statement, Mr. McLeod set to work fixing problems and nurturing strengths. To put his mission statement into action, he set up an elaborate advisory system in the Middle and Upper schools. Ten students meet with one teacher or administrator almost daily — the adult guides them, advises them and befriends them. "It has made the school more accountable to its students," said Mr. McLeod.

"You meet with them every day and you share their ups and downs," said Joanne Skertich, an advisor. "It is work. You constantly have to communicate with their parents and all their teachers. But it's worth it. Everybody gets noticed. And even after they graduate, there's a connection."

Mr. McLeod also hired more guidance counselors and learning specialists. And there is a Student Advocacy Committee that includes Mrs. Starr and Mr. McLeod, learning specialists, social workers, principals, deans and the nurse for each division. "We talk about every kid that needs help," Mrs. Starr said. "It gives us a lot of eyes."

Hiring Joan Starr, who had been a teacher elsewhere but had no experience in school administration, "was the best decision I've made in my ten years here," said Mr. McLeod. Although he was confident she could do the job, Mr. McLeod had to convince Mrs. Starr, a former trustee and a mother of two Newman boys, Barry '89 and Pierce '95. "The genuineness of her interest in kids, and her empathy and support for the kids, the faculty and the staff, are phenomenal," he said. "Everybody feels they can talk to Joan." Mrs. Baum called her "beyond words. She just really, really cares. She picks up every piece of the puzzle that's nobody's job description."

Another priority for Mr. McLeod has been to expand upon Mr. Lacopo's mission to increase diversity. He is very proud of his progress: during his tenure, Newman's minority student population has increased from twelve percent to nineteen percent. He would like to see that doubled. "Then you can say this is a meaningfully diverse community." And he would like to see more minority teachers.

But already, there has been a change in attitude. "Day to day, kids are mingling much more," he said. Of course, racism still exists — in the world and at Newman. In the late nineties, STEP — Students To Explore Prejudice — was formed to raise awareness of intolerance and celebrate diversity after racist graffiti were found scrawled in a Newman bathroom. Racial issues were a big topic for students in the nineties — again, a reflection of national trends — and STEP has provided an organized outlet for discussion. Even slights that have gone on forever — such as outsiders calling the school "Jewman" — are now discussed openly instead of simply being accepted as the norm. In 2000, Newman students organized the first Black History Month assembly at Newman. "Mr. McLeod has done a great job as far as increasing diversity, and helping Newman appreciate diversity of people and cultures," said Michael Walker '99.

"What I would say Scott has done for the school is clarify what has always been Newman's mission," Mr. Lapeyre said. "It has never been a school for rich, exclusive kids, at least not in philosophy. It was a school for Jewish orphans that also wanted the best and brightest kids. Scott has taken that foundation and integrated it very clearly with a focus on the individual, which I think Newman has always been about."

Much has happened during Mr. McLeod's tenure. When he first arrived, President Bill Clinton was in the White House, Edwin Edwards was in the Louisiana governor's mansion, and New Orleans had just elected Marc Morial mayor of New

STEP — *Students To Explore Prejudice* — *seeks to raise students' awareness of racial and ethnic prejudices. The club is comprised of students of all backgrounds.*

Orleans. Former football great O.J. Simpson was charged with murdering his ex-wife and her friend. *Cheers* and *Seinfeld* were the new hit TV shows, roller blades were the new hot accessory and white, middle-class kids were falling in love with rap and hip-hop. A medium called the Internet was a favorite newspaper topic, but it remained a mystery to most Americans.

In 1994, following her creation of an impressive hallway display celebrating Newman's ninetieth birthday, Genie Everett McCloskey '65 became the school's first archivist. With family friend and longtime Newman business manager, Martin Macdiarmid, Mrs. McCloskey searched every closet, cabinet and attic room in every building, unearthing long-forgotten Newman treasures. There was much to be found, including an elegant silver vase, blackened with age, which now shines brightly at special school functions. Only after Mr. Macdiarmid convinced her that no door had been left unopened did Mrs. McCloskey set about the daunting task of organizing ninety years of photographs, *Pioneers*, *Greenies*, newspaper clippings and memorabilia. "He always found a way to fund the things I wanted to do," Mrs. McCloskey said. "He was with me all the way as I established the archives."

Also in 1994, there was intense media coverage of Peyton Manning's final year as a Greenie and his choice to continue his education and football career at the University of Tennessee. Omar Douglas '90 signed with the New York Giants. After more than thirty years at Newman, Coach Tony Reginelli announced he was taking a year off. In his honor, the Anthony Reginelli Chair in Physical Education was established.

The student Executive Committee launched Wonder Week, a week of non-traditional classes taught by students and faculty. Courses have included sushi making, television news

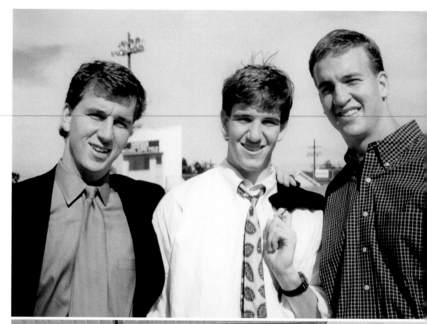

TOP: *The Manning brothers — Cooper '92, Eli '99 and Peyton '94.* BOTTOM: *A Wonder Week event on Lupin Field.*

*A hallway display celebrating Newman's ninetieth birthday.*

*Photo by Sean C. Smith*

production and car mechanics. "I taught about the connection between poetry and music," said Ketica Guter '02. "We explored how to take a poem and put music to it, or take the music away from a song, and find it is actually a poem." Miles Clements '02 taught "Who Really Belongs in the Kitchen?" Boys and girls learned the basics of cooking, and along the way, they learned a thing or two about gender roles. "Wonder Week is so unique and interesting — anything goes," he said. Hunter Pierson said he found it remarkable that the teachers and administrators were willing to put so much faith in the students. "They were allowing us to take the lead and pursue the somewhat radical idea that students could become teachers and explore this diverse set of subjects," he said. "I can't imagine many schools having that much conviction in their students."

In the mid-1990s, the trustees invited four faculty members — the headmaster and a representative from each division — to join the Board of Governors as full voting members. Around 1995, Mr. McLeod and the Board of Governors stepped up efforts to incorporate computers into every class. "We made a very, very major expenditure in technology and we basically wired the school," said then-Chairman Philip Claverie. "We were among the first schools in town to have a program aimed at improving teaching and not just having a lot of fancy equipment." Increasing the presence of technology on campus was part of a three-pronged Master Plan. The other two components were to increase the endowment for financial aid and faculty salaries and to make improvements to the campus.

In 1999, work began on the most extensive construction project in Newman's history. The new additions to campus include an improved dining hall; a new focal point and entry onto campus, the Gottesman Entrance and Lawn, and a new Lower School complex. The Lower School is made up of new playgrounds and open spaces and three separate but connected buildings. Two are new: the David Oreck Building and the Percival Stern Early Education Center, which includes the Lupin Kindergarten and replaces the old Stern Building. The third, the building at the corner of Jefferson and Loyola avenues, has been refurbished and named for Doris Zemurray Stone '26. The campaign to raise funds for these improvements turned out to be the most successful ever for Newman. Managed by former board chairmen Jay Lapeyre and Harry Blumenthal, *Newman 2000* raised $18.4 million over a period of seven years.

Newman acquired an international flavor that pervades all divisions. "The students represent as broad an international diversity as any school in the country," Mrs. Starr said. And students in all divisions are encouraged to learn about other cultures. The fourth grade stages Windows on the World, where each child is responsible for a presentation on some aspect of a particular country. They dress in indigenous clothing and serve native dishes, and they must deliver a report from memory. "It's a great opportunity to practice getting before a group and making an oral presentation," said fourth-grade teacher Joellen Welch. The Middle School language department organizes an international festival. And the Upper School's student-run Cultural Awareness Club puts on Culture Fest, which takes advantage of the many nationalities represented in the Newman student body by hosting an international lunch. The curriculum also celebrates the many cultures of its students: Newman now teaches five languages.

In 1998, Newman introduced a set of core values: respect, responsibility, honesty and integrity. Like the mission statement, the values serve as a simple reminder of Newman's essence. In the Lower School, as children are learning how to get along

*Jan Aronson Hall in the David Oreck Building.*

*ABOVE: Painting by art teacher Ruth Mullen.*
*BELOW: Painting by Alice Green '03.*

with each other and make their way in the world, the core values are emphasized in activities, games and other learning exercises.

In 2001, Susan Good became the first female chair of the Board of Governors. She joked about the pressure she felt as the trailblazer for all future women. "If the experiment doesn't work, I've ruined it for the female population," she said. Mrs. Starr said, "She is the only woman I can think of who could possibly have been the first woman to serve as board chair. She embodies every personal quality and every leadership characteristic we would ever want, and she is the sort of person and the sort of leader we hope our kids will grow to be."

Meanwhile, Newman students were into Ultimate Frisbee, large sport utility vehicles, and facial hair for the boys. In 1999, Ketica Guter brought a mascot back to Newman. "My sophomore year, I was like, 'Where's our mascot?'" she said. "So I got an alligator outfit and I was the Greenie Gator." The mascot remained alive and well after she graduated in 2002.

And in 2000, Fine Arts Week debuted. Every spring, Newman's halls fill with art and its stages and patios come alive with music, drama, poetry and dance. In 2003, a technologically savvy slide show set to music showcased student and faculty paintings and photography. The vibrant colors in the paintings of Alice Green '03 echoed Henri Matisse, and art teacher Ruth Mullen's stylized irises and swamp laurel had amazing texture and depth. At the show's end, students presented Mrs. Mullen with a large bouquet of flowers, "for being a great teacher and a great friend."

On September 11, 2001, Newman, along with the rest of the world, was rocked by the news that airplanes had been hijacked and slammed into the Pentagon and the two towers of New York's World Trade Center. "It was really hard," said Miss Guter.

*I was in a class at the time and then I saw every-body walking the halls. People were in a frenzy. Honestly I didn't believe it — I thought it was a joke. Then we saw it on TV in the library — a teacher wheeled a TV out for this. We gathered around and people called their family members in New York and D.C. And then our hearts were hurting because it was our country and our fellow Americans. Teachers were very lenient about let-ting us watch the footage.*

On Friday, September 14, Newman students gathered on Lupin Field for several minutes of silence facing a flag flying at half staff. That year, students raised $7,000 for the Red Cross.

It has indeed been an important decade for Newman: the school redefined its mission, strengthened its dedication to core values and grew the campus sub-stantially. "This is a very invigo-rating time for Newman," said Harry Blumenthal, the 2003–2004 Distinguished Alumnus. "I think the kids like it better."

Next, Mr. McLeod would like to work on the curriculum. "It is too congested," he said. "We've added so much but we haven't eliminated anything." And, he said, there is room for improvement in the integration of tech-nology across the curriculum. Finally, the physical plant still needs upgrades. Class space is inadequate, and Newman is run-ning out of property to develop, he said. There are also some maintenance issues to be addressed.

The Board of Governors met in the fall of 2003 to study

*CLOCKWISE FROM TOP LEFT: Dale Smith, geometry teacher and Dean of Students and Associate Principal in the Upper School. Coach Nelson Stewart '95. Mike Jackman, Middle School math teacher. Suzanne Schneidau, Middle School teacher and English department chair. RIGHT: The Distinguished Alumnus Award, given annually since 1990–91.*

where Newman should be in 2020. And a committee of students, faculty, parents and alumni is conducting a five-year study of the Upper School. Fortunately, Mr. McLeod said, the school has fixed the most serious problems and is now fine tuning. "We've addressed the immediate needs and concerns," he said. "We're dealing from strength now."

Discimus Agere Agendo. The hundred-year-old motto has remained a touchstone; for even as Newman sprints toward the future, there is always a firm foothold in tradition. "It was my experience with student government, with Wonder Week and with Summerbridge that allowed me to discover a passion," said Hunter Pierson. "And that is what Newman's motto — We learn to do by doing — is all about. You learn about education through teaching. You learn about government through student government. You learn about social change through Wonder Week, because it was the students who pushed to create it." Kate Barron sees the Humanities course as the curriculum's way of honoring the ideal of learning to do by doing, and in honor of the school's centennial, she had the class of 2004 study the period of 1853 to 1903 and called it "The World of Isidore Newman."

Favorite teachers from eras past — Dave Prescott, Pierson Marshall and Sheila Collins, to name just a few — continue to inspire new generations. But there are many new favorites as well, teachers hired by Mr. Lacopo and Mr. McLeod who often wittingly or unwittingly pick up and build upon old Newman traditions. Just as John Aker made Shakespeare come alive in the 1950s, today, English teacher Ann Sayas and English department chair Suzanne Schneidau are making it come alive for a new generation. For their final "exam," eighth-graders act out *Romeo and Juliet*, with each section of the class taking on different scenes. They make their own costumes and choreograph sword fights and dance scenes, and they create PowerPoint presentations about Shakespeare and his work.

Using gardening and harvesting as a teaching tool, Zelia C. Christian began a tradition of sparking an interest in science in young minds. Today, Lower School science teacher Jennifer Williams has a garden — and a home for her pet, Duckie Surprise — just outside her classroom in the new Oreck Building. Inside, she helps children as young as five years old conduct laboratory experiments such as creating an explosive concoction that blows the lid off a film canister. "They squeal and scream and cling to my leg and then say, 'Let's do it again!'" Mrs. Williams said.

A new generation of teachers is relating to students on their level, the way Wayne Frederick once did. Mr. Pierson said Dale Smith and others "revolutionized my way of seeing things." When Miles Clements took Mr. Smith's "unusual" geometry class a few years ago, Mr. Smith asked students to compare the relative value of Euclid, the founder of geometry, and basketball icon Michael Jordan. Geeta Karnik '98 said she and other students often had lunch or dinner at Taqueria Corona with Mr. Smith. "He and some of the other younger teachers were so approachable," she said. Ryan Skertich '01 called science teacher Randy Zell "awesome. You could go to his apartment and talk about stuff besides science and academics. You didn't want to *not* study or not do the homework, because you didn't want to let him down." Like the coaches that came before him, Coach Nelson Stewart was described as "like a father" by Brooks Nicolas '03 in his commencement speech. Middle School math teacher Mike Jackman shows a genuine and personal interest in his students, much as math teacher Bob Pfister did in the sixties and seventies. A former basketball coach, Mr. Jackman shoots baskets with students,

*The new Lower School, dedicated in 2003.* CLOCKWISE FROM THE TOP LEFT: *Bart Park with the David Oreck Building, the Percival Stern Early Education Center and the Lupin Kindergarten in the background. The Sydney and Walda Besthoff Foundation Entrance to the Percival Stern Early Education Center. Fourth Grade's Windows on the World display in Jan Aronson Hall. The Yarrut-Fishman Entrance to the Doris Zemurray Stone Building and the David Oreck Building.*

which gives him a way to connect with them outside the classroom. "I'm also a letter writer," he said. "I send kids letters offering support or congratulating them — whatever I can do to help them along." Linda Gottesman Baum said she remembers Mr. Jackman's genuine excitement for her son when things went well for him. "He was really interested in my son and really happy for him," she said.

Mr. Cooksey's theater tradition is alive and well in all divisions of the school: there are even operettas from time to time. Ginger Guma stages an impressive Middle School musical each year. In 2003, *The Wizard of Oz* featured a strutting, confident wicked witch — Mia McClain '07 — and a Dorothy — Aimee Gaubert '08 — whose pitch-perfect voice had no trouble reaching the back row.

The school has honored Isidore Newman's desire that music always be a part of the curriculum. Music is everywhere: students sing in choruses in all divisions, music finds its way into seniors' Humanities projects, the band is stronger than ever and a string group has developed in recent years.

May 16, 2003 is the last day of school for Newman seniors. They come wearing T-shirts from their future colleges and universities: Brown, Harvard, William & Mary, University of Georgia, Tulane, Syracuse, Texas. From 1999 to 2003, Newman sent 425 students to 119 different colleges and universities. In a morning assembly, Philip Cossich, president of senior class, presents the class gift — new senior patio furniture — "For next year's seniors and all the seniors to come."

Bobby Ragsdale, chairman of the executive committee, sighs as he prepares to give his final speech. He steps forward in dirty sneakers and an Army t-shirt; he is headed to West Point in the fall. He recalls walking into this auditorium on his first day at Newman, his freshman year. He was on scholarship and he came from what he describes as a poor family on the West Bank.

"I've been to more schools than I can remember sometimes, and to say this one is unlike any other is to say the bare minimum," he says.

*Newman is such an unusual, phenomenal, awesome school. The way this school functions and comes together is awe-inspiring.*

*Newman will echo throughout your entire life. Newman will follow you; it stays with you. Seniors, you have given to this school in ways you cannot know. I thank you for it, the school thanks you for it and Mr. Newman thanks you for it. Be proud of what you've done, and be proud to go to Newman.*

*But yet, here we are . . . In just a few more days — a few more hours, for all intents and purposes — I will no longer "go to Newman." This is something that for me, and most of you in the front rows today, has not sunk in yet, nor will it for a while. But it will. Someday. Someday soon, you will be lying in your room, staring at your ceiling, about to drift off to sleep, and you will realize that it's over — that you aren't coming back, that there are people — close friends — that you may never see again. But don't cry because it's over. Smile, because it happened.*

The seniors then pile into three buses and head to Mid-City Lanes to celebrate. Maya Alexander, who is going to LSU in the fall, reflects on highlights of her years at Newman. She was elected as a sophomore to ACTIONS, a community service group. They do service work all year, including a turkey drive to collect money to make Thanksgiving dinners for the mainte-

The Wizard of Oz, *staged in 2003 by the Middle School.*

*Former board chairmen Daryl Berger '65 and Jay Lapeyre '71.*

nance staff. They conduct can drives, collect Christmas toys and participate in walks for charity. This year, ACTIONS made spaghetti and served it at a New Orleans mission. Miss Alexander says she and her fellow students were overwhelmed by how grateful the mission staff was for their contribution. "They were so genuine," she says. When it was over, a member of the kitchen staff asked if they could all pray together. It was a large group of students, and it was an awkward moment — the kids were of different religions. But they agreed, and he asked them all to hold hands while he prayed. The prayer was powerful and touching: the man told the Newman students they were the future, he told them how important they were and how special their act that day was. Miss Alexander couldn't help crying, and many younger students were inspired to devote even more time to community service.

As the seniors bowl and drink Cokes, they pose for group pictures that some day will look as dated and nostalgic as old *Pioneer* photos look today. When they return to school, they sit in the cool dark of Henson Auditorium and watch a slide show of their lives at Newman. Then it is time for one final Newman tradition: they dash out to the senior patio and spray each other with whipped and shaving cream and water guns while they count down the seconds to the last bell. Lowerclassmen stand by, as do a few moms, who wipe away tears as they try to keep a discreet distance. Janine Moreau, who spent thirteen years at Newman, says what her classmates must be thinking: "It's so sad — it's all over!"

Perhaps the highest compliment one could pay to Newman comes from alumni who have become Newman parents. "Your kids are really taken care of, with love and concern, and, as they get older, they're challenged," said Valerie Besthoff

*Science Quiz Bowl, 2003.*

Marcus '78, a board member, mother of three Newman children and a member of a four-generation Newman family. "All the kids now seem so wonderfully self-possessed when you talk to them. They're all so proud of themselves and they're doing their own thing. I think it's great."

And this observation came from Merritt Lane '79: "It appears to me that Newman has retained the many wonderful aspects of its past, and yet is an even better place for educating my children."

Children of alumni say they value the tradition of attending their parents' alma mater. "I think it's great that my dad went there, I went there, and now my siblings are there," said Miles Clements '02. "We all experience the same thing, but at the same time, you can find your own place. There's always

room for you to find your own place. And there's such a sense of community — I still go back and talk to the old teachers and Miss Karen in the kitchen, and the maintenance men. They all remember me."

Alumni and former board chairmen Darryl Berger and Jay Lapeyre see a thread in Newman's history, one that stretches back to its founding. Mr. Lapeyre said:

> *Newman is a place where achievement-oriented kids from all over the city can come and be successful, providing they share common values. These values are very independent of religion, independent of gender, independent of race. The school is invariably focused on personal achievement: intellectual, extracurricular, and achievement related to self-esteem and development. And most importantly, the school is now taking achievement to a new level, recognizing those who are morally ambitious.*
>
> *Because we're not religious, because we have both genders, we can be a model for the city, to show that the balancing forces of the city are not race, but values. This is the foundation that Scott is leaving.*

"I think Newman is absolutely one of the key anchor institutions of this community," Mr. Berger said. "The fact that we have a prep school that can stand tall with the finest schools in America is an important thing in New Orleans. And it's more important now within the community, because we're educating a diverse student body. Newman is about gathering the very best kids you can, without regard to religion or circumstance, and in the modern era, without regard to race. That's remarkable.

"Entering on merit, succeeding on merit — that has always been the theme."

# SOURCES

## BOOKS

The Association for the Relief of Jewish Widows and Orphans. *The Story of the Jewish Orphans' Home of New Orleans*, New Orleans: The Association for the Relief of Jewish Widows and Orphans, 1905.

Barry, John. *Rising Tide*. New York: Simon & Schuster, 1997.

Birmingham, Stephen. *Our Crowd: The Great Jewish Families of New York*. New York: Harper & Row, 1967.

Brocato, Ron. *The Golden Game: When Prep Football was King in New Orleans*. New Orleans: Arthur Hardy Enterprises, 2002.

Fairclough, Adam. *Race & Democracy: The Civil Rights Struggle in Louisiana, 1915–1972*. Athens, Georgia: The University of Georgia Press, 1995.

Garraty, John A. and Carnes, Mark C. eds. Vol. 16 of *American National Biography*, New York: Oxford University Press, 1999.

Heller, Rabbi Max. *Jubilee Souvenir of Temple Sinai, 1872–1922*. New Orleans, 1922.

Jewish Historical Publishing Company. *History of the Jews of Louisiana*. New Orleans: The Jewish Historical Publishing Company, 1905.

Korn, Bertram Wallace. *The Early Jews of New Orleans*. Waltham, Massachusetts: American Jewish Historical Society, 1969.

Malone, Bobbie. *Rabbi Max Heller: Reformer, Zionist, Southerner, 1860–1929*. Tuscaloosa: The University of Alabama Press, 1997.

Rogers, Kim Lacy. *Righteous Lives: Narratives of the New Orleans Civil Rights Movement*. New York: New York University Press, 1993.

Rubin, Harold, ed. *Century of Progress in Child Care: Jewish Children's Home, 1855–1955*, New Orleans: Jewish Children's Home, 1955.

## COLLECTIONS/UNPUBLISHED DOCUMENTS

Historic New Orleans Collection, Francis Soyka papers.

Jewish Children's Home, Collection, 1870–1967. Collection number 180. New Orleans: Tulane University, Special Collections.

Archives of Isidore Newman School.

Andrus, Olive. "Isidore Newman School and the Manual Training Movement," thesis for Tulane University, 1938.

Jones, Mina. "The Jewish Community of New Orleans: A study of social organizations," thesis for Tulane University, 1925.

## NEWSPAPERS AND PERIODICALS

*The Daily Picayune*
*The New Orleans Item*
*The New Orleans States*
*The Times-Democrat*
*The New Orleans Times-Picayune*
*New Orleans CityBusiness*

## VIDEO

Cohen, Brian, director, producer. *Pushcarts and Plantations: Jewish Life in Louisiana*, New York: Apple West Productions, 1998.

*Children at play in Greentrees, the beloved playground.*

# INDEX

*Note: Italic page numbers refer to illustrations.*